Praise for *A Menagerie of Mysterious Beasts*

"Ken Gerhard's writings are always replete with original research and hitherto-unpublished reports. *A Menagerie of Mysterious Beasts* is no exception—a monstrously good, thoroughly entertaining, and highly informative read for cryptozoology fans everywhere!"

—Dr. Karl P.N. Shuker, author of
A Manifestation of Monsters

"Ken Gerhard deftly blends authentic historical accounts with piles of new eyewitness reports to create a heady, global cocktail of cryptid mysteries."

—Linda S. Godfrey, author of
American Monsters

"After reading this menagerie of the damned you will be in no doubt that monsters are real."

—Richard Freeman, author of
Dragons: More Than a Myth?

"Ken brings us an excellent read, a combination of his own personal investigations and direct eyewitness testimony. Importantly, the book flows very well as it deals with a variety of cryptids, including more controversial subjects which he is to be credited for not shying away from."

—Adam Davies, cryptozoologist and explorer

A MENAGERIE OF
MYSTERIOUS
BEASTS

About the Author

Ken Gerhard (San Antonio, TX) is a widely recognized crypto-zoologist. He has traveled around the world searching for evidence of mysterious animals, including Bigfoot, the Loch Ness Monster, the Chupacabra, flying creatures, and even were-wolves. Ken has authored three books on the unexplained, and his research has been featured on the History Channel, Travel Channel, Syfy, National Geographic, A&E, truTV, Nat Geo Wild, Science Channel, and Destination America. He is a regular guest on *Coast to Coast AM*.

ENCOUNTERS WITH CRYPTID CREATURES

A MENAGERIE OF
MYSTERIOUS
BEASTS

KEN GERHARD

Llewellyn Publications
Woodbury, Minnesota

FIRST EDITION
First Printing, 2016

Cover background image: Shutterstock.com/13703339/©mythja
Cover illustration: Dominick Finelle/July Group
Cover design: Kevin R. Brown
Editing: Lauryn Heineman
List of interior art credits on page 215

Llewellyn Publications is a registered trademark of Llewellyn Worldwide Ltd.

Library of Congress Cataloging-in-Publication Data
Names: Gerhard, Ken, author.
Title: A menagerie of mysterious beasts : encounters with cryptid creatures / Ken Gerhard.
Description: First edition. | Woodbury, Minnesota : Llewellyn Publications, 2016. | Includes bibliographical references.
Identifiers: LCCN 2016020032 (print) | LCCN 2016032295 (ebook) | ISBN 9780738746661 | ISBN 9780738749273
Subjects: LCSH: Animals, Mythical. | Monsters.
Classification: LCC GR820 .G47 2016 (print) | LCC GR820 (ebook) | DDC 001.944—dc23
LC record available at https://lccn.loc.gov/2016020032

Llewellyn Publications
A Division of Llewellyn Worldwide Ltd.
2143 Wooddale Drive
Woodbury, MN 55125.2989
www.llewellyn.com

Printed in the United States of America

Other books by Ken Gerhard

Encounters with Flying Humanoids: Mothman, Manbirds,
Gargoyles & Other Winged Beasts
Big Bird!: Modern Sightings of Flying Monsters
Monsters of Texas (coauthored with Nick Redfern)

Contents

INTRODUCTION

In past centuries, persons of nobility would maintain and exhibit awe-inspiring collections of rare and exotic animals, which had been gathered from faraway lands. The ostentatious displays were often regarded as shows of great wealth and influence, but they also served another important purpose. In a world that seemed dark and mysterious, these bestiaries would enthrall and fascinate curious observers, reminding them that remote corners of the planet still harbored fabulous beasts that they could scarcely imagine.

Charlemagne, the mighty emperor of Western Europe, was among the first to possess such a menagerie during the Middle Ages. In 802 CE the caliph of Baghdad presented the ruler with an Asian elephant named Abdul-Abbas. Elephants were a genuine novelty in Europe at that time, and the majestic giant remained in Charlemagne's care for eight years until it expired, all the while astonishing all who saw it. Other intriguing specimens that Charlemagne kept on display included lions, monkeys, and bears.

During the early part of the thirteenth century, King John of England began to exhibit remarkable animals on the grounds of the Tower of London. The Roman emperor Frederick II gifted John's heir (Henry III) three leopards in the year 1235, and sixteen years later the king of Norway provided him with a polar bear to add to the impressive collection. The Tower's menagerie ultimately spanned six centuries and included hundreds of strange and fascinating creatures. One notable beast was Old Martin, a grizzly bear donated by Canada's Hudson Bay Company to the English Monarchy in 1811. Ultimately, there was a tragic incident in 1830, in which an old lion named George escaped his enclosure and engaged in a bloody battle with two captive tigers in an adjacent pen. The ensuing public fallout effectively heralded the end of the Tower's royal menagerie.

Not to be outdone, France's aristocracy had an impressive menagerie too. King Louis XIV began to assemble his collection at Versailles in 1664. A century later, one of its most celebrated inhabitants was an Indian rhinoceros that resided on the palace grounds for twenty-two years, until it was slaughtered by disenchanted rebels amidst the chaos of the French Revolution.

During the nineteenth century, as the general public became aware of startling advancements in science and exploration, traveling menageries consisting of all manner of extrinsic animals would tour Europe and North America, taking in handsome profits for their owners. Crowds of people would line up and pay a respectable fee for the opportunity to gawk at unusual specimens that they had never seen before. Surely, the result of such expositions was that they served to stimulate people's imaginations in previously unimaginable ways.

It is in keeping with this spirit that I present you, the reader, with this compendium of fabulous beasts—my very own virtual menagerie, if you will. The esoteric creatures described within these pages remain strictly relegated to the world of myth and legend for now, yet there exist compelling accounts by people who've claimed to have actually observed these beasts with their very own eyes. And because amazing new species are still being catalogued with alarming regularity, it is my firm hope that in due time some of these "monsters" will earn their rightful place in the annals of zoology. Or perhaps even in an exhibit where they can awe and inspire like the uncommon animals of ages past. It is my ardent hope that you will marvel at this astounding assemblage of mysterious beasts as other menagerie enthusiasts have throughout history.

Chapter 1
THE MINNESOTA ICEMAN: A CHINESE APE-MAN?

During the summer of the American Bicentennial, the aroma of corn dogs and funnel cakes permeated the air of the Minnesota State Fairgrounds. The festive sounds of carnival rides and circus music echoed as a young boy wandered throughout the crowd. Suddenly, his attention was drawn to a barker's voice resonating through loudspeakers ahead. "Is it man, or is it beast? What is it—a caveman from our prehistoric past? The legendary Bigfoot?" Within moments, the boy located the source of the announcement, an eighteen-wheeler that had been converted into a sideshow attraction. On its outer walls, colorful posters hinted that whatever was housed inside was not quite human.

The boy approached cautiously, overcome with curiosity but also hesitant—fearful that whatever was on display just might inspire future nightmares that he could scarcely fathom. Eventually, he gathered up his courage, took a deep breath, and handed the price of admission to an older man standing at the entrance.

As the youth slowly made his way up the long, wooden ramp to the doorway of the trailer, he could feel his excitement mounting and his pulse quickening. Upon entering the chilly and tight enclosure, he discovered a crowd of people gathered around a glass-covered coffin in the center of the room and gawking at the figure within, which was evidently encapsulated in a block of ice. The boy squeezed in between two adults, stood up on his tiptoes, and peered down at the manlike shape frozen within the centerpiece. The thing, whatever it was, appeared to be covered in short, brown hair and displayed a startling death grimace on its monstrous face. Seemingly halfway between man and ape, the being's true nature was a genuine mystery.

Truth be told, that young boy was none other than yours truly, so the so-called Minnesota Iceman possesses a special, personal significance for me. That incident was one of many seminal events in my early life that put me on the trail of enigmatic beasts. Now, whether you believe that the Iceman affair merely represents one of the greatest hoaxes in history or you are convinced that its very existence validates the survival of archaic, hair-covered subhumans to modern times, its existence spawned undoubtedly one of the most fascinating and significant sagas in the annals of cryptozoology.

Our tale begins with the late Frank D. Hansen of Rollingstone, Minnesota. As early as 1967, Hansen was traveling around the United States to various fairs, livestock shows, and carnivals, exhibiting what appeared to be a deceased, furry, humanlike being entombed in a block of ice, which in turn was housed in a refrigerated glass sarcophagus. His advertisements did not state precisely what the anomaly was, suggesting that it might be some type of primitive man while also implying that it could just as easily be a fabricated model, similar to the "mermaids" that had been cobbled together by Japanese taxidermists for centuries by combining the body parts of assorted animals like monkeys and fish.

Beginning on November 28, 1968, the exhibit was visited multiple times by Terry Cullen of Milwaukee, a zoology student and budding herpetologist and veterinarian. Cullen felt that whatever was being displayed was a real flesh-and-blood creature, not a fake. He realized the importance of bringing it to the attention of scientists and tried in vain to get various academics to take notice, though he did finally convince one anthropology professor at the University of Minnesota to go and take a look. After exiting the trailer, the professor walked away utterly speechless, according to Cullen, and seemingly didn't want to venture a guess as to what the Iceman might actually be.

Coincidentally, the late Dr. Grover Krantz, an eminent physical anthropologist heralded as one of the pioneers of Bigfoot research, was also attending that very institution. Krantz later wrote, "One aspect that grates on me is that if I had walked just a little bit farther at the Minnesota State Fair in the summer of 1968, I would have been the first scientist to see the damned thing." According to an episode of the 1990s television series *Unsolved Mysteries*, two experts who did manage to "see the damned thing" around that time period were a zookeeper named Bob Surpleski and an environmental researcher named David Rivard. Both men came away convinced of the Iceman's authenticity, though they apparently took no action.

Eventually, Terry Cullen got in touch with Ivan T. Sanderson, a famous author, biologist, animal collector, and ethnographer who was running the Society for the Investigation of the

Unexplained out of his home in New Jersey at the time. Cullen phoned Sanderson on December 12, 1968, and expressed his opinion that the Iceman was some type of unknown hominid. Ivan was skeptical at first but felt that Terry seemed both knowledgeable and sincere; thus, he decided to drive out and take a look for himself. It just so happened that, at the time, Sanderson had a houseguest—none other than the father of cryptozoology, Dr. Bernard Heuvelmans of the Royal Belgian Institute of Natural Sciences, who had dedicated his life to the pursuit of unknown animals. Sanderson tracked down Frank D. Hansen and convinced him that both he and Heuvelmans should be allowed to examine the specimen in person.

The scientists arrived at the Hansen homestead on December 16 and were permitted to undertake a superficial examination of the Iceman for three consecutive days, though they were only allowed to view their subject through several inches of glass and ice, which was largely opaque. During that time they took a number of photographs and measurements to the best of their ability and also questioned Hansen about the Iceman's origins. Hansen told them that the exhibit actually belonged to a mysterious, California show-business millionaire who had discovered the curiosity in a refrigerated warehouse in Hong Kong, purchased it for an undisclosed amount, and shipped it back to the United States.

Hansen initially told Sanderson and Heuvelmans that the Iceman had apparently been frozen in a 6,000-pound block of ice, which had been found floating in the North Pacific Ocean by Russian sealers, and that ultimately the thing had wound up in Hong Kong. Incidentally, his version of events changed multiple times as time went on. Months later, Hansen stated that the thing had actually been discovered by Japanese whalers and then by Chinese fishermen. Finally, in a 1970 article for *Saga Magazine*, he said that he shot the creature himself while hunting in the Northwoods of Minnesota. A year earlier in June of 1969, a tabloid had published a story about a female camper who claimed she shot the Iceman in self-defense after it had molested her.

Regardless of how the Iceman reached Hansen, it is important to consider the physical characteristics of the specimen that Sanderson and Heuvelmans examined, based on their detailed notes. They both estimated that the being would have stood about six feet tall and would have been noticeably muscular and stocky, weighing around 250 pounds. Its entire body, except for its face, palms, and the bottom of its feet, seemed to be clothed in hair that was two to four inches long and had an agouti pattern, meaning that the individual hairs displayed stages of varying coloration in a pigmentation pattern that fades from darker tips to lighter roots. As far as primates go, this particular trait is only known to exist in certain kinds of monkeys.

For a number of reasons, both scientists ruled out the possibility of the Iceman being an excessively hairy human (*Homo sapiens*), such as a person of Japanese Ainu descent, or even one born with hypertrichosis (an exceptionally rare genetic condition of abnormal hair growth). The being did not appear to have a neck, and its shoulders and torso were broad and barrel-shaped. Its arms were longer than a human's, reaching almost to its knees, and its legs seemed longer than those of any nonhuman ape, indicating that it probably walked upright. It also displayed male genitalia. The most disturbing aspect was the fact that it appeared to possess two bullet wounds—one that had ripped through its left wrist, breaking its arm, and a head wound that had blown out both of its eyes. There also appeared to be a puddle of blood underneath its head. The Iceman evidently met a tragic end.

While the true shape of its cranium couldn't be determined, there wasn't an exaggerated brow ridge visible, and the forehead sloped only slightly backward. The flesh on its face was a yellowish color, and the Iceman didn't display any sign of prognathism (a protruding upper and/or lower jaw) like an ape. Its nose was the most noticeable feature, prominent and pug shaped, with two large nostrils that faced forward. The eye sockets were unexpectedly round and rather large with both eyeballs missing. There appeared to be blood running out of one eye socket and possibly the remnant of an eyeball on its other cheek. The mouth was difficult to see, but the lips seemed to be rather narrow. The upper lip was peeled back to expose four large molars like those of an orangutan as well as a canine tooth that was not at all prominent like in other primates. There was a series of folds or wrinkles around the being's mouth that resembled the jowls of an elderly man and also a bit of hair resembling a mustache below its nose. Its ears couldn't be clearly seen.

The Iceman's hands were by far the most remarkable and outstanding morphological structures visible. They were enormous and bulky in comparison to its body and arms, though their linear measurements were within reason: about eleven inches long and seven inches across. Its thumbs were fully opposable (like a human's) but were remarkably slender and long. They also tapered towards the end rather than expanding. The knuckles were not well defined. It didn't have claws but rather copper-colored nails that seemed oddly manicured. One puzzling feature was enormous plantar pads on the outside of the hands that may indicate that the creature went down on all fours occasionally.

As with all species, the design of the Iceman's feet would be paramount in determining its true place within the taxonomic system of zoological classification. The hallux, or big toe, was adducted as in hominids and not at all opposed like in anthropoids, indicating a proximate relationship to humans rather than apes. Its feet were eight inches wide and squat, with the toes being essentially equal in size, creating a flat front. The toenails were yellowish and cropped. Sanderson wrote that the feet reminded him of fossilized Neanderthal tracks from a cave in Toirano, Italy, and that they also bore characteristics that reminded him of Bigfoot tracks that he had examined while in northern California. He noted that such feet would have been ideal for traveling over the snow.

Perhaps the most troubling part about the Iceman's physiology was that it didn't really resemble anything from our known fossil history. Nonetheless, Heuvelmans felt strongly that it probably represented a living Neanderthal man. Sanderson disagreed with his colleague's assumption, believing the Iceman to be a complete unknown. Primatologist Dr. John Napier of the Smithsonian Institute later stated that the Iceman, if genuine, was distinct enough to represent an entirely new clade in the superfamily of hominids. He also pointed out that the Iceman displayed the worst traits of both men and apes, making it an unlikely evolutionary design.

*Meg Buick's interpretation of the Minnesota Iceman
as it may have appeared in life.*

Despite its odd features and Hansen's duplicity, Sanderson and Heuvelmans were both convinced that the Iceman itself was not a fabrication but rather an authentic flesh and blood specimen that had been alive within the prior five years. This was despite the fact that studying the thing had been problematic, since over half of the ice that it was encased in was cloudy, restricting a clear view of its entire anatomy. Obviously, they were not able to touch any part of the subject, nor extract any hairs or tissue samples from it. Hansen had told them that such samples had been sent to top experts initially, but he never delivered on his promise to provide Sanderson and Heuvelmans with any resulting data or precise names or details. One of the things that convinced the scientists that the Iceman was real was the fact that they both claimed to have smelled its decaying flesh coming up through cracks in the ice after accidentally shattering the glass lid of the coffin when they placed a hot lamp on top of it. Both men also felt that the creature's state of decomposition was causing discoloration of its skin as well as the formation of gaseous bubbles in the ice around it.

Assuming for a moment that the original Minnesota Iceman was genuine, where did it really come from? Heuvelmans would later theorize that it might have had its origins in the nation of Vietnam. From Indochina's dense montane jungles, there have been historical accounts of primitive, hairy men referred to as the *Nguoi Rung*, which in Vietnamese means "forest people." Heuvelmans speculated that Frank Hansen, who served as a fighter pilot during the Vietnam War, could have conceivably smuggled its corpse into the United States by concealing it within a body bag. There are stories about American soldiers stationed in Vietnam who occasionally encountered and shot aggressive, manlike animals that they called Rock Apes.

My friend and colleague John Kirk, who lived in Hong Kong for many years, informed me that it would have been downright impossible to smuggle something like the Iceman into that city during the 1960s. However, I can't help but wonder if there is some truth to Hansen's initial statement about it ending up in a Hong Kong warehouse. After all, there are some truly striking similarities between the Iceman's appearance and descriptions of the Chinese wild man referred to as the *Yeren*. Moreover, there have been multiple reports of Yeren being either captured or killed in the decades leading up to 1968. Most of the alleged incidents stem from the central part of China, which consists of vast, forested mountain ranges.

In one instance, three different witnesses corroborated a capture, which apparently took place in the year 1922. The local militia paraded a sturdy, six-foot, captive wild man through their village one day. All three men later recalled that the thing had been covered in dark, red hair and that it possessed extremely large hands and feet. Additionally, a traveller named Wang Zelin observed what appeared to be a hair-covered "wild woman" that had been shot by hunters in Gansu Province during the 1940s. One could hardly hope for a better eyewitness, since Zelin was evidently a trained biologist. In a Chinese magazine article published in 1979, he later reminisced, "It was tall, about two meters... The cheekbones were high, making the eyes deep set... The shoulders were rather broad... The hands were very big with long fingers ... The feet were over a foot long and six to seven inches wide."

A similar incident occurred in the jungles of Xishuangbanna in Yunnan Province during 1961 when a wild man was said to have been shot by railroad workers. Some Chinese scientists dismissed the account, stating that the subject in question was most likely a large gibbon. But an anthropologist and Yeren investigator named Zhou Guoxing uncovered some testimony that the specimen had in fact looked more like a man than an ape. Since no one is sure what happened to its remains, it's not impossible that they could have ended up on ice and transported to Hong Kong, where they remained in deep freeze for a few years.

A close encounter that includes a detailed description and which paints a favorable comparison to the Iceman occurred in June of 1977. A villager named Pang Gengsheng claimed that he came face to face with a Yeren on the eastern face of Mount Taibai in Shaanxi Province. While the man was intently cutting firewood, the creature surprised him, backing him up against a stone cliff wall with nowhere to retreat to. Gengsheng later told investigators,

> [The being was] about 2.1 meters tall, with shoulders wider than a man's, a sloping forehead, deep-set eyes, and a bulbous nose with slightly flared nostrils. He had sunken cheeks … and round eyes also bigger than a man's. … His front teeth were as wide as a horse's. … His whole face, except for his nose and ears, was covered with short hair. His arms hung down below his knees. He had big hands and fingers about six inches long. … He walked upright with his legs apart. His feet were each about a foot long and half that width … with splayed toes. He was male. That much I saw clearly.

After an hour-long stand off, Gengsheng picked up a rock and hurled it at the intruder, which grunted in disgust and wandered off.

Later that same year, a young man in the Shennongjia region logged another report. During the month of August, Xiao Xingyang allegedly had seen a hairy man-beast spying on him from the forest. "I then saw its face very clearly. It looked like a very thin old man, with protruding teeth, sunken eyes, and upturned nose. I was very frightened and ran away instantly."

Due to the similarities in descriptions, it would appear that China's Yeren is the same species as Vietnam's jungle-dwelling

Nguoi Rung and also Mongolia's *Almas*—a mysterious hominid said to dwell in the Altai Mountains. Despite the suggestion by British anthropologist Myra Shackley that these hairy primitives are of *Homo neanderthalensis* (Neanderthal) stock, perhaps it would be more reasonable to link them to *Homo erectus* instead. Ice Age fossils of *Homo erectus* have been discovered all over Asia, and it's not completely beyond the realm of possibility that a tiny population of descendants still survives, inhabiting remote wilderness areas. As Shackley herself points out, in terms of longevity *H. erectus* was the most successful human ancestor, with a reign of almost two million years. *H. erectus* fossil finds have also been widespread, indicating that the species was highly adaptable. Of course, one could certainly make the argument that the Minnesota Iceman doesn't match perfectly with reconstructions of *H. erectus*, but there are many gaps remaining in our knowledge of our fossil history. Who's to say that the Iceman might not be an evolutionary side branch on the seemingly bushy tree of human evolution? Only a thorough examination of the actual body would answer these questions.

At the conclusion of Heuvelmans and Sanderson's three-day evaluation, Hansen asked both scientists not to publicize any of their findings. (We know this not only from Sanderson's writings, but also because Hansen later confirmed it). Despite that request, Heuvelmans published a scientific paper on the Minnesota Iceman in February of 1969, and by May Sanderson had penned an article for *Argosy*, the magazine of which he was science editor at the time. Apparently, Sanderson had also mentioned the Iceman in passing while appearing as a guest on *The Tonight Show* with Johnny Carson. As a result, their claims caused quite a sensation and even garnered the attention of the Smithsonian Institute in Washington, DC, and possibly even the FBI.

Clearly feeling pressure, Hansen vanished for a few months and then resurfaced, claiming that he had commissioned a sculptor to construct an exact latex replica of the Iceman with which he would now be touring instead, while the original specimen was placed in storage. This bizarre turn of events, along with the fact that Frank Hansen continually changed his story through the years, makes a compelling argument that the entire affair was a monumental hoax. Was Hansen merely a scam artist, a brilliant showman who deserves to be ranked among the likes of P. T. Barnum?

It would seem that the revelation of a "composite" Iceman was enough for the Smithsonian to declare the whole affair an obvious hoax, particularly after they had spoken with a Hollywood special effects designer named Howard Ball who took full credit for the creature's design.

But Sanderson and Heuvelmans later noted at least fifteen differences between the replica Iceman and the original specimen that they had studied at Hansen's residence. I confirmed this fact in a phone interview with a man named Richard Grigonis, who had worked with Sanderson during the late 1960s. Sanderson had requested that Illinois resident Grigonis take some photos of the 1969 version of the Iceman at that year's International Livestock Exposition in Chicago, for comparison purposes.

The saga of the Minnesota Iceman contains some intriguing subplots. For example, during July of 1969, Frank Hansen was detained at the US border for several days after displaying the Iceman in Canada. Customs officials were concerned because his exhibit so closely resembled a human cadaver. Hansen insisted that the thing was merely a latex model, but when officials requested a sample of its "skin" as proof, he flatly refused, stating that it would cause irreparable damage to the exhibit. Hansen was so distressed that he even called Sanderson for advice. Sanderson suggested that Hansen allow officials to x-ray the Iceman replica so that they could see that it lacked a skeletal structure. Hansen rejected this suggestion, saying that "the owner" would never allow it. Ultimately, Hansen called in a favor and was allowed to reenter the country with his exhibit. (Intriguingly, that favor was granted by none other than the state senator and future vice president of the United States, Walter Mondale.)

There's also the matter of the mysterious show-business millionaire who Hansen credited with actual ownership of the Iceman. If he was not merely an invention of Hansen's, it is possible that he was Hollywood screen legend Jimmy Stewart. Stewart was known to have a keen interest in subjects like the Abominable Snowman or Yeti, due to his friendship with millionaire adventurer Tom Slick of San Antonio, Texas. Slick had actively pursued evidence for mysterious animals around the world, and Stewart certainly would have had the influence needed to get the Iceman past Customs and into the United States. Moreover, it is said that the Iceman's owner was a very religious man, which Stewart is believed to have been, and didn't want to be the one who toppled the biblical theory of creation. It is possible that the iconic actor was genuinely interested in how people would react to the Iceman, but he apparently also stated that he would dump its body back into the Pacific Ocean if it were ever to become a divisive issue.

In 1974, Bernard Heuvelmans coauthored a book with famed Russian hominologist Boris Porshnev titled *L'homme de Néanderthal est toujours vivant,* in which they laid out a case for the Iceman representing a surviving Neanderthal, labeling it *Homo pongoides,* or "apelike man." Heuvelmans never wavered from his belief that the subject that he and Sanderson had examined for three solid days had been genuine. Sanderson passed away in 1973 and also stuck to his guns until the very end, believing that the original Iceman had been some type of Abominable Snowman. During a telephone interview with Bigfoot researcher Al Berry in 2002, Hansen was asked what he thought the Iceman represented. Hansen responded that whatever it was, he definitely did not associate it with Bigfoot. However, in 2005, Hansen's widow Irene told investigator Curt Nelson that she and Frank had once traveled to California to visit with Roger Patterson and his wife. Patterson is famous for a controversial film that he shot of an alleged Bigfoot creature in northern California during 1967, but why the visit? Either two of the great hoaxers in history wanted to drink a toast together, or Hansen was looking for answers.

Frank Hansen died in 2003, taking the secrets of the Minnesota Iceman with him to his grave. His exhibit incidentally continued to tour the United States for over a decade, visited by tens of thousands of people, including me.

It is believed that the Hansen family had sold the Iceman off after Frank's passing, perhaps tired of all the turmoil it had created in their lives. The oddity had evidently been in the possession of a Minnesota company that specializes in supplying spooky props to theme parks and haunted attractions.

However, over the past couple of years it has resurfaced in quite a dramatic fashion due to the actions of a Texan by the name of Steve Busti. Steve is owner and curator of Austin's *Museum of the Weird*, a colorful exhibition that proudly displays a variety of curios, including shrunken heads and a cyclopean piglet. Like myself, Busti first saw the Iceman as a young boy, and it sparked a lifelong passion for both carnival-style freak shows and cryptozoological mysteries.

During the early part of 2013, the Iceman replica appeared on the auction website eBay with a hefty asking price of $20,000.

Busti contacted the seller and purchased the exhibit (including the original, glass-covered display coffin and Hansen's promotional posters) for an undisclosed amount. He then arranged for its transportation to his museum in Texas, and the strange journey was featured on a television show called *Shipping Wars*. As part of that particular episode, Lyle Blackburn, Chris Buntenbah, and I, all Bigfoot researchers, met up with Busti and a film crew near Fouke, Arkansas, which is famous for sightings of another hairy, manlike monster that was the inspiration for the 1970s cult classic film, *The Legend of Boggy Creek*. Blackburn, Buntenbah, and I were possibly the first researchers to get a glimpse of the Iceman in this century, and we also led Busti and his truck-driving costar into the swamp in order to demonstrate how Bigfoot fieldwork is typically conducted. After the program aired that summer, Busti arranged for a grand premiere of his new, prized museum exhibit and invited me to give a lecture recounting the history of the Iceman. As part of the event, small groups of enthusiastic visitors were escorted into a refrigerated room where the coffin containing the Iceman was being housed. The saga had come full circle: I once again found myself peering down into the face of an enigma. Though I recognized the subject as the same one I had viewed some thirty-seven years earlier, a lifetime of experience allowed me to now carefully examine the thing with a scientific eye.

I was able to come to a rather abrupt determination. In my humble opinion, the object that I was looking at did not appear to be organic in any way. It was obviously a latex model of some sort—there was no conceivable way that two trained scientists could have come to the conclusion that this thing had ever been alive, especially after three days of careful examination, ice or no ice. I confirmed that this was indeed a replica. Frank Hansen had taken one of the most important scientific discoveries of the twentieth century and had parted ways with it or hidden it where it may never be found.

All these years later many questions remain. Although, for me personally, it really all comes down to this: Could two eminent zoologists like Heuvelmans and Sanderson have made such an obvious misjudgment? If so, it rocks the very foundation of the field of cryptozoology, since these men were the discipline's iconic founding fathers, and such a glaring blunder would provide ammunition to skeptics who view researchers like myself as romantic crackpots. And if the original Iceman was authentic, what ultimately became of its remains? Were they really placed in storage, and where? Were they dumped in the ocean? Was Hansen understandably fearful of serious legal ramifications, given that he had a humanlike corpse with bullet holes in his possession? At this very moment, the remains of the original Minnesota Iceman may be resting in an unmarked grave somewhere out there…waiting to captivate us once again.

Steve Busti with his Minnesota Iceman exhibit.

Chapter 2
APE-MEN IN THE AMERICAS

The Duende and Sisemito of Central America

In the previous chapter I mentioned author Ivan T. Sanderson, who spent a great deal of his life investigating and writing about natural mysteries. While my personal interest in zoological enigmas dates back to my childhood, it was as a freshman in high school that I first discovered one of Sanderson's most influential books in the student library. Ultimately, that particular volume had a tremendous impact on me—I checked out that copy so many times over the course of my tenure that the head librarian eventually gave it to me as a graduation present. The compendium was titled *Abominable Snowmen: Legend Come to Life*, and for it, Sanderson had undertaken a masterfully thorough census of elusive, mystery hominids from various points around the globe, including many lesser-known and obscure ones. In addition to North America's iconic Bigfoot (or Sasquatch), he discussed the infamous Yeti (or Abominable Snowman) of the Himalayas, the Neanderthal-like *Almas* of Central Asia, and the diminutive *Sedapa* (or *Orang Pendek*) of Sumatra, as well as similar types from Africa and South America. But he mentioned one other cryptid creature that really piqued my interest.

You see, for a time Sanderson and his wife had taken up residence in the tiny Central American nation of British Honduras (modern-day Belize) and had gained the solemn trust of many of the locals. Sanderson repeatedly heard stories about rarely seen, forest-dwelling pygmies known as Duendes, who were typically encountered near the edge of the Maya Mountains in the nation's southern interior. The term *Duende* is a Spanish word that essentially translates to "elf" or "goblin," and most Belizeans seem to regard these mischievous beings as magical imps not unlike the mythical little people featured in fairy folklore around the world. In Belizean stories, Duendes are typically portrayed as tiny, bearded men that sport large hats and carry tiny machetes or clubs. Furthermore, they are said to lack thumbs on their hands, to have backwards-pointing feet, and to abduct unsuspecting children from time to time. This description seems familiar and most assuredly has some connection to the fairy lore of Europe. There are, after all, distinct Spanish and British influences apparent in Belizean culture.

Sanderson had apparently also spoken with reputable forestry officials who confided in him that they had actually seen small, unfamiliar hominids emerging from the fringes of the montane forests. Sanderson explained,

> These little folk were described as being between three foot six and four foot six, well proportioned but with very heavy shoulders and rather long arms; clothed in thick, tight, close, brown hair looking like that of a

short-coated dog; having very flat yellowish faces but with head-hair no longer than the body hair except down the back of the neck and mid back. Everybody said that these Dwendis have very pronounced calves but the most outstanding thing of all about them is that they almost always held either a piece of dried palm leaf or something looking like a large Mexican-type hat over their heads.

The Duendes' tracks were easily recognizable because they featured extremely pointy heels, according to what Sanderson had been told. Furthermore, these hair-covered dwarves were said to be nocturnal and to make sounds like a baby crying. They also delight in wrapping their arms around cottonwood trees and grasping the hands of unsuspecting humans, according to my friend and colleague, cryptozoologist Richard Freeman. Belief in the Duendes apparently extends far to the north of Belize. On my most recent trip to Mexico, a farmer in the western state of Nayarit told me that he had once seen a Duende peering at him from between his cornstalks. When I asked him what it looked like, he described it as resembling a dwarf with a long nose.

I have always been intrigued by Belize. Here is a little jewel of a nation known for its thriving tourist industry centered on tropical Caribbean beaches and shimmering, turquoise water. But beyond its populated coastline lies a vast wilderness of lush, uninhabited jungles that are teeming with wildlife, waterways, and extensive cave systems. Impressive but overgrown Maya ruins pepper the landscape, reminders of an ancient empire that once boasted a population much greater than that which currently resides in the country. The romantic allure of those kinds of pristine, emerald forests seems to always beckon intrepid adventurers like myself. Legends of lost cities and monstrous, man-eating beasts still permeate the darkest and least inhabited regions of Mesoamerica, adding to the intrigue. In fact, a handful of explorers who successfully penetrated this domain returned to civilization with tales of primitive manlike creatures existing at a subhuman level and frequently abducting or even cannibalizing those who venture too deep. Perhaps Sanderson was on to something.

As an adult my dreams of a Belizean adventure were always obstructed by those irritating financial burdens commonly referred to as "bills," despite the relative accessibility of the place. Eventually, in 2004 I received a modest, unexpected inheritance and, recognizing a rare opportunity, quickly made plans to undertake the journey at last. My young wife at the time, Lori, was to accompany me on the trek, and we planned on taking advantage of the cooler winter weather. I'd decided to focus my efforts primarily on the Maya Mountains where the Duende was said to dwell. The trip would be a boon to Lori as well, as she had recently developed a keen interest in archaeology and was looking forward to visiting the impressive ruins of Caracol, which rests in the southern Cayo District.

We zeroed in on an area known as Mountain Pine Ridge not only because of its proximity to remote Caracol, but also because I remembered something that the late anthropologist Dr. Grover Krantz had once written. A colleague had pointed out to Krantz that sightings of Bigfoot-like creatures were always concentrated around areas where coniferous trees were prevalent. This seems to be supported by the fact that the vast majority of reports stem from higher elevations and rainforests, particularly in the Pacific Northwest of the United States and Canada, and a surprising number of accounts come from the pine thickets of the Deep South and Florida, whose local hominids are referred to as Skunk Apes. Krantz theorized that pine needles could provide a viable food source for nomadic hominids, particularly in the lean winter months, and that they could actually help them regulate their body temperature like an organic antifreeze. Since I conjectured that the Duende might be a pygmy-sized relative of its North American cousins, it seemed like as good a place as any to take up the search.

While laying the groundwork for my trip, I chanced upon an article that had been written by a researcher named Mark Sanborne. Sanborne, who apparently had been affiliated with the now-defunct International Society of Cryptozoology, had beaten me to the punch and had undertaken an expedition (similar to the one I was planning) over a dozen years earlier in 1992. Sanborne first spent considerable time in the Cayo District where the Duende is apparently well known. In addition to asking many locals about the subject, he had also uncovered some local books dealing with Belizean folklore.

Generally referred to as *Tata* (Papa) *Duende,* the most common depiction of a Duende portrays a tiny, manlike figure in tattered clothing displaying the features previously mentioned: long beard, large hat, four fingers, backwards-pointing feet, etc. Many people Sanborne spoke with claimed to have had spectral encounters with these beings. He came to the conclusion that Duendes were essentially perceived to be forest-dwelling spirits not that dissimilar to gnomes. However, he also mentioned that the eminent zoologist Alan Rabinowitz had written about seeing a small, manlike figure at the edge of Belize's Cockscomb Basin Wildlife Sanctuary while conducting pioneering work in the field of jaguar research. It is difficult to ignore the affirmation of such a skilled wildlife observer. Here is a description of the sighting from Rabinowitz's book, *Jaguar: One Man's Struggle to Establish the World's First Jaguar Preserve:*

On the fourth night I went out as usual to the hill. It was a particularly dark night because rain clouds hid the moon and stars. I put on the headphones and scanned the darkness for Xaman Ek's [a roaming jaguar] signal, moving the antenna in a full circle. There was no signal, but there was something else. I sensed something was wrong. Even wearing headphones I could feel a stillness in the forest around me. A chill ran down my back, and for an inexplicable reason, I felt frightened, unsure of the darkness.

Countless times I had tracked at night but never had I felt this way. I continued listening for the jaguar over the next half hour, but the feeling that something was wrong wouldn't leave. I decided to return to camp.

The truck was facing the forest. As I turned on my headlights and swung the truck around toward the timber road, a strange sight flashed before my right headlight. Standing at the edge of the forest, I had a brief glance at what looked like a little man, about three feet tall, holding his left hand up, palm out as if signaling me to stop.

My first reaction was terror. I had heard too many stories of the *duendes* of the forest. I raced down the road before deciding my imagination was getting the better of me. After driving two miles, I turned around went back to the site.... There was only a bush where I thought I'd seen the little man. Yet, an uneasy feeling, a tingling sensation came back to me stronger than ever. I didn't linger....

... It surprised me to learn how prevalent the belief in these little men was among most people I spoke with.

Rabinowitz had also written of a second, distinct mystery hominid that the Maya preserve caretakers told him about, *el Sisimito*. With descriptions of being much larger and more apelike than the Duendes, the Sisimito sounds virtually identical to North America's Sasquatch: it's a hulking, hairy, upright creature that leaves behind huge, humanlike footprints. One of Rabinowitz's workers told him this:

Dere also de big hairy man, the Sisimito, in de bush. Two men see he in Cockscomb already... You know de hairy man close when you hear scream at night, like woman screaming. Long time ago, an old man come from de south, he still a boy. He go wit he fadder way back in Cockscomb for hunt. He go different way from he fadder and soon hear crash in de bush. He tink maybe it a tiger [jaguar] and he get scared and hide in de big mahogany log, and look out from a crack. Den, a big hairy man come out from de bush and he have a big bird (hawk) in he hand. The hairy man bite off and eat de head of de bird. Then he go 'way. The man lay in de log and shake because he scared bad. Finally he fadder come out of de bush and dey both go 'way fast. De fadder see de hairy man too.

In *Abominable Snowmen*, Ivan Sanderson mentioned, in fact, that the Sisimito was well known in the highlands of neighboring Guatemala. But he was apparently unaware of its presence in southern Belize or else didn't mention it. Like a Duende, the Sisimito is said to only have four fingers as well as backwards-pointing feet (perhaps accounting for the difficulty in trying to track one) and evidently possesses a nasty disposition, often murdering native men and abducting young women à la King Kong. According to Sanderson, Guatemalans would typically know when the Sisimito had come calling because they would be inexplicably overcome with uncontrollable shivers of fright.

From what Sanborne was able to discern, most of the Sisimito accounts from Belize seem to be centered in the far south of the Toledo District, near a tiny Kekchi Maya village named Blue Creek. His inquiries into the matter there revealed that the monster is considered to be a rarely seen, flesh-and-blood animal (likened to a gorilla), which lives in caves in the high bush and has a piercing scream.

During 1994, cryptozoologist Marc E. W. Miller also visited Blue Creek village and uncovered more intriguing stories. A local man named Richard Genus claimed to have seen a Sisimito while working on a plantation just six years prior.

He described the thing as a six-foot, apelike creature and was apparently so traumatized by the experience that he had an emotional breakdown following the encounter. Based on his discussions with the locals, Miller was of the firm opinion that the Sisimito is an unknown, American ape that stands about as tall as a man and emits loud vocalizations that are distinct from those of howler monkeys, which are prevalent in the area.

There is further evidence that a type of undiscovered hominid may inhabit the jungles of Central and South America. During the late nineteenth century a colorful adventurer named Edward Jonathan Hoyt (better known as Buckskin Joe) claimed that he shot a five-foot, manlike creature as it climbed over the edge of his bunk one night while he was on a prospecting trip in Honduras. Brazilian writer Pablo Villarrubia Mausó chronicled other accounts of Honduras's Sisimito while traveling through that nation. An elderly man named Don Manuel Mejia related that he had encountered one of the creatures in the mountains of Pico Bonito during 1912. He recalled that the creature had been extremely tall and hairy and walked upright. Sanderson had a correspondent who mentioned a similar beast called the *Arrancalenguas* (Tongue Ripper), which was known for killing livestock near the border of Honduras and El Salvador. American diplomat, engineer, and ethnographer Richard Oglesby March wrote of a prospector who claimed to have shot a gorilla-like animal in Panama during 1920. The man described the thing as standing six feet tall and weighing around 300 pounds. It was covered in long, black hair. The prospector noted that its big toe was parallel to its other toes, like on a human foot.

*The author examines a large area of flattened grass
in the Maya Mountains of Belize.*

As far back as 1860, naturalist Philip Henry Gosse wrote about a great anthropoid ape that might exist in the nation of Venezuela. He noted, "On the cataracts of the Upper Orinoco ... [there are] reports of a 'hairy man of the woods,' reputed to build huts, to carry off women and to devour human flesh." According to explorer Alexander van Humboldt, the "hairy man" was known locally as the *Vasitri* (Great Devil). South America evidently has no shortage of Bigfoot-type beasts, and they are known by a variety of names, including *Mapinguari, Mono Grande, Ucumar, Maricoxi, Didi,* and *Shiru.* A controversial photo taken by Swiss geologist François de Loys in 1920 alleges to show a five-foot, upright ape, which he shot while on a Venezuelan expedition. Critics point out that the subject in the picture looks strikingly similar to a large spider monkey with its tail obscured. Regardless, the Green Continent exudes potential for new discoveries. As recently as 2013, a previously unknown species of tapir weighing almost 250 pounds was catalogued there for the very first time. It had been living inconspicuously in the grasslands of western Amazonia.

Lori and I landed in Belize in December of 2004. Due to the fact that the vintage tires on our rental jeep were ostensibly smooth, we endured a treacherous, rainy drive up slick, muddy mountain roads to our destination, a primitive lodge nestled atop the Pine Ridge of the Maya Mountains. We rolled in just after dark and were received by our host, an esoteric expatriate who had formerly been a colonel in the US Army. Richard seemed wholly amused by the purpose of our visit, as he viewed the Duende as nothing more than a native superstition, but he had been gracious enough to arrange a skillful guide for us, Honorio Mai. Mai is a native *chiclero* (gum collector) whose great uncle is famous for discovering the jungle-shrouded ruins of Caracol. According to Richard, Mai was one of the few men who had ever traversed the treacherous Rapaculo Pass alone—armed with only a machete, no less. Before turning in for the evening, we all enjoyed a memorable Belizean dinner that featured the most delightful tomato and orange soup imaginable.

Early the next morning, Mai drove us down the rugged, twenty-mile gravel road to the ruins of Caracol. On the way he explained that one of his sons had once been assaulted by an unseen stone thrower there: probably a Duende, he figured. We arrived at our destination and immediately climbed the many steps of the great pyramid of Caana, where we ate a lunch of sheep liver tacos that Mai's wife had graciously prepared for us. Mai then shocked Lori and me by informing us that his younger sister had once been kidnapped by a Duende! As he explained it, many years ago the two-year-old had been playing near the edge of the forest when she began to point and excitedly shout, "Look at that strange boy!" Apparently no one in her family was able to see the tiny being except for her. Immediately after that, she vanished mysteriously, later found alone in the jungle sleeping soundly next to a strange piece of fabric. When the material was taken as a bad omen and burned, Mai's family was dealt a tragic blow—another infant sister died suddenly of unknown causes.

For most of that afternoon, we hiked through the surrounding jungle canopy. My excitement became evident when we detected the unmistakable grunts of a howler monkey troop roosting nearby. Without hesitation, I instructed Mai to lead us directly to the source, and he wasted no time, hacking a pathway through the brush until we were standing just below them. Observing these impressive primates in the treetops above us was without a doubt one of the great thrills of my life, though the creatures did not seem very pleased to see us. We endured a barrage of their thunderous grunts while they shook the treetops, causing a shower of leaves to fall onto our heads.

Having failed to encounter a Duende at Caracol, we resolved to make the long drive down to the Cockscomb jaguar preserve the following day, which we did. This of course is the location where Alan Rabonowitz had his sighting years before. The thrill of finding myself standing among numerous fresh, crisscrossing trails of jaguar tracks is one that I will not soon forget. However, the fact that we never actually caught a glimpse of a jaguar (or any other animal) speaks to the denseness of the jungle there. At one point I began to make wood-knocking sounds (supposedly a Sasquatch-locating technique) in order to see if I could elicit a response. I did not hear anything answer back, but something very heavy abruptly crashed through the brush, just out of sight.

Our quest became slightly more promising when I interviewed a couple of caretakers who worked at the sanctuary. A younger man named Manuel told me that he was from the Blue Creek area and that he remembered his grandmother telling him that she had once heard the call of the Sisimito. She had said that it had sounded like a man yelling, only much louder. An older caretaker named Ignacio Pop then related to me that he had heard about a recent incident in which enormous, man-like footprints were found in the grounds surrounding a shrimp farm on the coast, a dozen miles to the southeast.

For the remainder of our stay in Belize, Lori and I decided to part ways with Honorio Mai and concentrate our efforts in the region around Mountain Pine Ridge, where we were based. Among the gadgets I had brought along were some motion-activated trail cameras, a video recorder with night-vision capabilities and a primate pheromone chip. This unique chip had been developed by clinical psychiatrist and avid outdoorsman Dr. Greg Bambenek, who combined the pungent essence of both gorillas and humans, thinking that the smelly concoction just might entice other hominids such as Bigfoot. (Despite being sealed in multiple layers of plastic ziplock bags, this particular item imbued an odor to my luggage that lingered on for many years to come.)

*Casts of mysterious, hominid-shaped footprints
found in Belize's Maya Mountains.*

In the end, my deployment of these gadgets over the next few days yielded no results whatsoever, though while scouting the area, we were amazed to stumble upon impressions in the ground that resembled small human footprints!

This notable event occurred on our first day hiking a trail along winding Privassion Creek. Lori first noticed a single track impressed in a tiny patch of white sand, and just a few yards away I discovered two other prints in some dirt among sparse weeds. These impressions admittedly lacked much definition. Toe marks were not vivid, though the tracks all displayed the general shape of a bare human foot. The two in the dirt were about nine inches long. Most startling was the fact that the single track in the sand was only six inches long and had a remarkably pointed heel, just as Sanderson had described the spoor of the Duende!

Though the prints certainly didn't make for conclusive evidence, I was encouraged by the fact that we were hiking in a remote, virgin area with limited accessibility. The nearest humans lived many miles away, and, besides, these tracks did not display the tread marks and distinct edges that would indicate footwear was involved. I cannot for the life of me think of any reason why someone would be walking around in that area barefoot with potential hazards like venomous fer-de-lance snakes and scorpions crawling about. Because I had brought along some plaster-like material known as UltraCal, I was able to make casts of two of the impressions: the one with the pointy heel and the clearer of the two in the dirt. With this find under our belts, we departed Pine Ridge.

Following a memorable visit to the scenic coast (specifically, lovely Ambergris Caye), Lori and I returned home to Texas. Word of the prints we found did cause a small stir in the Big-foot community. In hindsight, we were probably being a bit overzealous at the time, since the ambiguous casts fell far short of any standard of acceptable scientific evidence. However, we were intrigued enough to return to Belize a year later in order to mount a second expedition, which yielded minimal results. For the follow-up journey, I had intended to make it down to Blue Creek Village, since I felt that the accounts of the Sisimito were more compelling than those of the Duende. But finances were limited this time around, and we remained in the more accessible Mountain Pine Ridge for the duration of our stay. We had also considered crossing the border into Guatemala but were warned that it was not safe, as banditos were on the prowl.

Someday I hope to continue with more Central American research. Yet it's not always mandatory to travel to exotic, far-away lands for a dose of good mystery. Sometimes, it can be found in our own backyard.

Dwarves of the Dakotas

The notion of there being an undiscovered race of "protopyg-mies" (hair-covered, subhuman dwarves), as Ivan Sanderson labeled them, seems a bit outlandish on the surface. However, there is no denying the fact that these beings have reportedly been encountered at numerous locales around the globe. The best known of these is Sumatra's *Orang Pendek* (Little Man), whose existence is supported by the discovery of 13,000-year-old *Homo floresiensis* skeletons on nearby Flores Island. According to physical anthropologists that have studied these remains, the "hobbit" (as *H. floresiensis* has been nicknamed) seems to represent a pygmy-sized side branch of human evolution. Since 13,000 years is merely a blink of an eye in geological terms, could the Flores Man or something like it still exist? On the island of Sri Lanka, there is a legend about a race of shaggy, and apparently quite nasty, pygmies known as the *Nittaweo*. From Africa, we hear accounts of the tiny *Agogwe* and *Sehite*, and from South America, the *Didi* and *Shiru*. We mustn't ignore the possibility that Europe's abundant "little people" lore may have some bearing on the subject as well. The point is that behind every legend there may be a tiny grain of truth, and this particular grain seems to walk on two little legs.

What is utterly dumbfounding is the prospect that the protopygmies' range might even extend into the United States. Following a lecture that I gave in northern Minnesota, a Chippewa family from North Dakota that was in attendance approached me. They confided that their reservation had regularly been under siege by a race of generally unpleasant, savage, and hairy dwarves that had become quite a nuisance, primarily due to the fact that they are known to raid food supplies and small livestock from residents' properties. These entities are also blamed for carrying off a pet dog or two on occasion. The sincerity of this family was unquestionable, in my opinion, as they seemed awfully concerned about the situation.

Reminiscent stories are abundant. Across the border in Montana, the Crow Nation has a famous myth that refers to the *Nirumbee* or *Awwakkule*, described as powerful and ferocious dwarves with sharp teeth, short limbs, and potbellies. It is said that these beings inhabit the Pryor Mountains and that they are capable of raining stone-tipped arrows onto their enemies with great accuracy. Ancient petroglyphs attributed to the dwarves speak to their antiquity. Other tribes share remarkably similar tales: Idaho's Nez Perce tell of the *Itste-ya-ha*, which are the *Hecesiiteihii* to the Arapaho and the *Jogah* to the Iroquois. In addition, I once uncovered an obscure reference to the *Goga'ne* of Oregon (possibly an Umatilla name, though I'm not sure). There is also the shared belief that these "cannibal" dwarves are keen on human flesh and have been around as long as the Native Americans.

While speculation into these matters may seem like utter fantasy, we need only to reflect once again on the tiny Flores Man as well as the explanation offered by its discoverers that it quite possibly represents a dwarfed subspecies of *Homo erectus,* a highly widespread human ancestor that thrived on three continents for almost two million years. Although there is no evidence that *H. erectus* ever managed to reach the Americas before its presumed extinction 70,000 years ago, one cannot completely discount the possibility of a diminutive version migrating to the Americas at some point ... and that small groups of them live on.

Houston's Hominid

It is not uncommon for me to hear from people who believe they've had experiences that extend well beyond their capacity of understanding. The following is an example of one such incident that was brought to my attention by a colleague who resides in my old haunt of Houston, Texas. Consequently, I conducted two separate and in-depth phone interviews with the primary eyewitness, Justin Myers. Here is his story.

On Sunday, April 3, 2011, Myers and his girlfriend went jogging at Terry Hershey Park on the city's west side. As they often did, the couple ventured off the main path and into the surrounding woods for a brief nature hike. While following a slight, meandering creek, they came upon a felled tree in front of a bend. Just beyond that was an overgrown grotto carved in the muddy bank of the steep creek bed. Squatting within the grotto was what they at first took to be a very tall person wearing a hoodie and kneeling down at the water's edge.

As the couple stopped and watched, they began to realize that the being did not appear to be human. It was covered from head to toe in matted hair; its relatively small, hair-covered face featured enormous, round, dark eyes like those of a pug dog. The apparition seemed startled by the couple's presence and began to run away very fast. Myers and his girlfriend were understandably terrified and immediately began to run in the opposite direction, back the way they had come. His girlfriend was bordering on hysterics by the time they had made it back to their vehicle. Despite the distance they had put between themselves and the thing, they still felt an eerie vibe, as if they were being watched.

Myers and his girlfriend finally did muster up the courage to return to the scene of their encounter several days later, but only while accompanied by my initial contact, a Fortean researcher named Jason DeVries. The group discovered what appeared to be strands of long, dark hair hanging from a nearby tree branch, in addition to a half-eaten fish where the thing had been squatting down. There was also something that resembled a footprint in the mud. They did not find any other evidence but took a few photographs of the location. DeVries later told me that he felt uncomfortable while at the scene and thought that he heard some low-pitched grunting and wood-knocking sounds in the distance. He also detected a foul odor in the air.

While most readers are by now filing this account away into their personal Bigfoot dossiers and calling it a day, I should point out that Myers emphasized that the pug-eyed creature was noticeably slender and that its seemingly lifeless arms hung limply by its side while it ran away, significant details that are not typically associated with the well-chronicled archetype of the traditional Sasquatch. It is therefore unclear to me precisely what kind of creature the couple actually encountered, though it must be acknowledged that hirsute hominids of varying shapes and sizes have been reported all over the world. On the outskirts of America's fourth largest city, an exceptionally bizarre example may be lurking just on the fringe of civilization.

Manticores: Four-Legged Beasts with Human Faces

A mere thirty miles northeast of New Orleans along the Pearl River corridor lays the vast Honey Island Swamp. Considered to be one of the most impenetrable wilderness areas remaining in North America, it is also alleged to be home to a hairy man-beast known as the Honey Island Swamp Monster. While its descriptions are reminiscent of Florida's Skunk Ape as well as Arkansas's Fouke Monster and other bipedal Bigfoot creatures said to stalk southern bottomlands, I interviewed one eyewitness who had an exceptional encounter with a quadru-ped version.

RobRoy Menzies's interpretation of Bigfoot as a quadruped.

At the time of his sighting, Louisiana-native Herman Broom was only fourteen years old. He and a fishing companion were boating up the Pearl River when they saw the creature. Broom explained,

> The one I saw was on all four legs: face like a man, body like an animal … very scary. It was about the size of a medium-sized man. Brownish in color, dirty brown. Fur not long, one-inch maybe. I did not see ears. Face hair-free. Eyes similar to a person. No protruding snout. Flat face. Did not notice a tail, nor do I remember seeing the feet. Flat back. No odors or sounds. It was not aggressive.

Almost seemed like it wanted to say something. But it put fear in this fourteen-year-old boy at the time. For many years we never talked about what we saw in the woods that day. Who would believe us?

Well, quite possibly Bigfoot researcher Wes Ison, since he claims to have encountered a similar beast in Laurel County Kentucky some years later. With Ison's kind permission, I reproduce his story here:

In 2005, while four-wheeling with my girlfriend in some bottomland where I live, I was following the Laurel River as it snakes its way through these dense bottoms. It was getting dusk dark.... I was carrying my Sony Hi8 camcorder because I have seen Bigfoot before, but it had been awhile. I also had my .44 Magnum pistol on me, for we have lots of wildlife around here and I would rather be safe than sorry. As we continued our ride, we came to a bend in the creek and the tree frogs and crickets were so loud that they about drowned out the ATV's engine roar. So I turned it off so we could hear them better because the sound was just really nice and soothing.

As we sat and listened, I caught a movement out of my right eye, so I turned to see an animal which looked like a gorilla for it was on all fours but was the color of an orangutan ... an orange/red, and when it turned its head to look at me its face, which I saw pretty well, was white much like that of a skull. My girlfriend was looking the other way when I jumped off the ATV to film this creature. The creature moved quickly to the base of a downed treetop, which it was in front of and just climbed right over onto the other side where I lost sight of it. My camera was around my neck, so I popped off my lens cap cover and started filming... [but] all I got was a short video of the main branch of the tree shaking where it had just went over. This all took place in just a few seconds, possibly twelve to fifteen seconds. I was very disappointed, as I'm sure anyone who looks for these creatures would be.

While it should be noted that the overwhelming majority of Bigfoot accounts describe a bipedal, upright primate that strides like a human, reports of them going down on all fours do exist, particularly in the swampy terrain of the southeastern United States. Some researchers have theorized that there might be a distinct quadruped subspecies, indigenous to these low-lying swampy areas. Cryptozoologist Loren Coleman proposed an alternative identity, referring to these creatures as "Napes" (North American Apes) and suggesting that they could represent a surviving population of Dryopithecines, ancient pongids that inhabited the temperate forests of Europe millions of years ago during the Miocene epoch.

White Bluff Screamer

Throughout the hills and hollers of northern central Tennessee, there exists colorful folklore that speaks of a monster known as the White Bluff Screamer. As with most local legends, descriptions of this particular creature seem to vary widely depending on who you ask. Yet most of the old-timers will tell you that it is said to be a tall, shaggy, white, three-toed creature with a long neck and flat face that has acquired a taste for both dogs and livestock. In 2010, a woman I'll call Brenda related a brief encounter to me that might lend a measure of truth to the tale.

> Me, my friend, and her sister went camping at this place out in the middle of nowhere with our kids. It had a nice place to swim. It got late and our fire went out. We didn't have tents, so we slept in our cars. My friend and I were about asleep when my friend's sister, who had parked right behind us, turned on her headlights and yelled to us to turn on ours. What we saw were two big, dirty, white, hairy things that stood six feet tall or better and were slightly hunched over. It was only a split second we saw them before they were gone. They moved extremely quickly. My friend and I saw two of them, and her sister had seen four when she yelled at us. We have no idea what we saw, but it made me think of all the stories I had heard growing up. We didn't stay. We went home.

During my follow-up interview with Brenda, I elicited additional details from her: "It was about ten to twelve years ago when we saw them. My dad thinks it may have been between the Hickman, Maury, and Williamson County lines, at a swimming hole called Mill Seed. It may be on South Lick Creek Road or Schoals Branch Road. Not quite sure, but that is the area."

I should point out that Williamson County has produced a handful of Bigfoot sightings over the years, including a report from South Lick Creek from the early 1970s as well as a report of a gray-colored ape-man that crossed the road in front of a vehicle in 2010. Also, high-pitched screams are some of the most common vocalizations associated with Bigfoot creatures. Accounts of gray- or white-haired Sasquatches are less common but not unheard of. Possible explanations for this type of pelage include a genetic condition such as albinism, or perhaps like the hair of other animals, theirs simply tends to lose pigmentation as they grow older. If this is the case, the deep woods of central Tennessee may harbor a veritable retirement community for excessively vocal Bigfoot creatures.

Chapter 3

WEREWOLVES AND OTHER CRYPTID CARNIVORES

The mammalian order Carnivora consists of some 280 known species, many of which are superbly adept at remaining hidden. Crafty and elusive, these animals stealthily stalk their prey, waiting for an opportune moment to pounce on their unsuspecting victims, often invoking a quick and silent death before vanishing into the surrounding brush. In the grand scheme of things, it's really not that long ago that big cats, bears, dire wolves, hyenas, and a host of other apex predators hunted our human ancestors on a regular basis. Consequently, we have developed a healthy fear of these types of creatures and like to think that we're intimately familiar with all of their forms. Surprisingly, once in a while we discover something entirely new.

As recently as 2006, scientists first confirmed the existence of a new species of sizable predator on the island of Borneo—the Sunda clouded leopard (*Neofelis diardi*). These fair-sized cats can weigh over fifty pounds but are rarely ever seen. The Bornean bay cat (*Pardofelis badia*) was photographed for the very first time in 2003, and a distinct, new subspecies of felid called a tigrina was found in the Brazilian grasslands during 2013. Earlier that year, a previously unknown carnivore named the olinguito was detected in the rainforests of Ecuador. Occasionally, American mountain lions (*Puma concolor*) are spotted in areas where they have been declared long extinct. Other unidentified predators could be out lurking in the shadows somewhere, waiting to strike.

La Bête du Gévaudan: A Famous French Werewolf

A blood-curdling howl pierces the dead of night as a full moon looms overhead. In the mist-shrouded forest, a sinister beast prowls, patiently anticipating its unwary mark wandering into its kill range. Suddenly and without warning, the menacing monster snarls and lunges, baring its razor sharp teeth and long claws—an agonized scream, then silence. This scenario may sound eerily reminiscent of a typical Hollywood thriller or perhaps even a gothic novella. But according to copious official archives, a minimum of sixty victims were devoured by something that was referred to as a bona fide werewolf two and a half centuries ago in rural southern France.

It was a turbulent time in France during the 1760s. Great political unrest and religious conflict abounded. Apart from the privileged minority or those in the favor of King Louis XV and the Roman Catholic Church, the vast majority of the citizenry was impoverished and persecuted. A series of brutally harsh winters added to the desperate conditions, and starvation was looming in the more remote regions. One such place was Gévaudan, a pastoral, mountainous region in the south of France. The greater part of the region's inhabitants were simple farmers who were disenchanted by the high taxes imposed by the king and cut off from Paris, causing them to be vulnerable to attacks from Spain.

During the summer of 1764, the killings began. On June 30, a woman named Jeann Boultet was murdered near the town of Les Hubacs. A few days later, a fourteen-year-old girl was devoured at Habats, and just over a month after that, a fifteen-year-old girl was found dead near the village of Masmejean. By the end of August, the attacks became a regular occurrence. Most of the victims were young, generally girls or boys who were charged with tending to flocks of sheep or small herds of cattle in remote, wooded areas while the men worked the fields. The descriptions of the assailant (given by those who were fortunate enough to escape molestation) were consistent: it was an imposing, wolflike animal with a huge head and gaping muzzle, erect pointy ears, pronounced fangs, and an elongate tail with a tuft of fur on the end. It was said that the beast's powerful body was covered in reddish fur, with a black stripe running down the length of its back. Its ferocity was unprecedented, as the creature regularly decapitated, disemboweled, or otherwise mutilated its human victims, yet it strangely avoided livestock.

As the body count mounted, so did the hysteria throughout France. The king responded by dispatching brigades of soldiers and professional wolf hunters to the region in order to slay the creature. The abusive soldiers only served to inflame the local citizenry's festering disdain for the monarchy, while the hunters bagged a couple of exceptionally large wolves, which they blamed for the killings. But the attacks didn't cease. Ultimately, the bloody reign of *la Bête du Gévaudan* lasted for almost three years.

Finally on June 19, 1767, a social outcast named Jean Chastel dispatched the monster, allegedly by firing a single silver bullet that had been blessed by a priest. Chastel claimed that he had been engaged in prayer just moments before and that the beast had wandered into a clearing right in front of him, as if God had answered. The animal's remains were paraded through village streets for a couple of weeks, after which its smelly carcass was presented to King Louis, who insisted that the putrid cadaver be disposed of immediately. In recognition for slaying the creature, Chastel was handsomely rewarded and became a legitimate folk hero. But almost two and a half centuries later, the actual nature and identity of the Beast of Gévaudan remain a mystery. It is widely believed that its body was buried in an undisclosed location.

During the summer of 2008, I had the good fortune of traveling to France in order to revisit the case. It was all part of a two-hour television special titled *The Real Wolfman*, which was being produced for the History Channel. For the purpose of the program, I was paired with a police homicide investigator named George Deuchar. Many experts, including the late French cryptozoologist Jean-Jacques Barloy, felt that the killings attributed to the Beast of Gévaudan were, in retrospect, likely perpetrated by a human serial killer either disguised as a wolf or perhaps using a trained animal in order to do his bidding. Another theory holds that the monarchy took advantage of the mayhem incited by increasing wolf attacks and used it to instill a feeling of helplessness throughout the populace in order to maintain control. Deuchar and I were charged with exploring the various theories about the true nature of the beast.

The experience was remarkable, to say the least. In addition to visiting the Gévaudan region (now called Auvergne) and the precise locations of some of the attacks, we were led to the exact spot (by one of Jean Chastel's descendents, no less) where the beast met its end. Patrick Soulier, curator of a local museum dedicated to the monster, granted us access to many of the original archives and death certificates from the period, and we also had an opportunity to observe France's tiny remaining wolf population at a wildlife reserve.

In Paris I was able to confer with cryptozoologist and Beast of Gévaudan expert Jean-Jacques Barloy, and, most importantly, to meet with a taxidermist named Franz Julien at the National Museum of Natural History. Julien had apparently made a fascinating discovery over a decade earlier. In 1997, he had uncovered an old document that indicated that the Beast of Gévaudan's remains were displayed at the Paris Zoo until 1819—and that zoologists concluded that they were those of a hyena!

While this notion may sound utterly fantastic (modern hyenas are native to Africa and Asia only, not Europe), there is an argument to be made for this possibility. The French have historically had a strong presence in Africa, and it was not unheard of for animal collectors of the eighteenth century to have such a creature in their menagerie. Who's to say that a captive hyena couldn't have escaped or been set loose into the French countryside? Ravenous and desperate, the animal conceivably might have attacked solitary humans on occasion, as African specimens are known to do. While hyenas actually belong to a completely distinct family, they do superficially resemble wolves and other canids. And they are seriously formidable predators, reaching weights of up to 150 pounds and possessing bone-crushing jaws. Hyenas can be found on the snowy slopes of Mount Kilimanjaro, so one could have potentially survived the harsh winters of France for a time. A species of enormous cave hyena (*Crocuta spelaea*) was in fact common in France around 10,000 years ago during the Ice Ace, though the probability of any of these surviving until the eighteenth century is remote. It would not have been the first time in history that an out-of-place animal achieved legendary status.

Statue of the Beast of Gévaudan at Saugues, France.

Like most cryptozoological enigmas, the mystery of the Beast of Gévaudan is a complex one, and the mass hysteria of the period no doubt compounded the issue. One of the world's preeminent cryptozoologists, Dr. Karl P.N. Shuker (who holds a PhD in comparative physiology and runs the website *ShukerNature*), summed it up beautifully in an e-mail to me: "I think that this is a case of composite identity, involving several different inputs, including an unusually large wolf, rumors of an escaped hyena, and human killer(s)." Or perhaps a werewolf actually was terrorizing France over two centuries ago … if you believe in such things.

Nebraska Wolfman

Following my appearance on a television special, *The Real Wolfman*, I was contacted by a Nebraska resident named Brad who related the following to me:

> I saw your show about the wolfman over in France. I have seen that creature on Interstate 83, while driving south in Nebraska. It came up on me on the highway. I was stopped by a law enforcement officer for about five minutes, and when I left the scene, I was going slow enough. It was on the other side of the freeway. I saw it coming toward me. Its eyes were yellow, and it was huge, and it was coming at me at a good pace. I was so startled that I floored my pedal to the metal and never looked back. It's the honest-to-God truth!

Subsequent attempts to gather more details from Brad have been unsuccessful. But while Nebraska is practically the last place on Earth where we would expect to hear about werewolves trotting around, my good friend and colleague Linda Godfrey of Wisconsin has amassed a sizeable number of so-called Dog Man accounts from numerous locales around the United States. She has also written a handful of excellent books suggesting that something resembling both hominid and canid may indeed exist. The issue is whether or not this is a corporeal phenomenon involving biological specimens, or, rather, spectral manifestations of apparitions that are wholly supernatural.

Poland's Wilkolak

Robert Tralins was a prolific author who penned over 200 books dealing with otherworldly topics. Many of the anomalies he claimed to have researched first-hand were featured as factual narratives on the popular television show *Beyond Belief: Fact or Faked*, which aired from 1997 until 2002. Additionally, Tralins once won a $750,000 libel lawsuit against the King of Egypt after he had been accused of making things up about the ruler, so the general consensus is that Tralins's info was legitimate.

In his 1970 publication *Supernatural Strangers,* Tralins told the story of a Polish couple who claimed they were besieged by a *wilkolak* (werewolf) on their very own property during the evening of June 7, 1963. At that time, Josef and Sava Zbojno resided in the village of Wilczyn, which is situated in central Poland. Hearing their dogs acting up one full-moon night, the couple went out to investigate the matter. The pooches' disposition quickly turned from aggressive barking to hiding and whimpering. That's when Sava resolved to approach the enclosure and check on the dogs as her husband Josef illuminated the yard by opening the front door to their cottage.

Suddenly and without warning, there was a horrifying howl, just as a menacing beast with glowing eyes and razor-sharp fangs appeared. The grotesque monster seemed to be a huge wolf that was standing upright and cloaked in the tattered garments of a peasant. In a state of sheer panic at this point, Josef grabbed a wooden club and sprinted to his wife's defense, smacking the apparition as hard as he could and happily causing it to retreat into the shadows. Regrettably, the husband's action had been a moment too late, as the werewolf had managed to scratch Sava, leaving a deep gash. Despite their concern that they would not be taken seriously, the couple reported the incident to local police. According to Tralins, the Wilczyn Wilkolak had been seen on prior occasions, particularly when the moon was full. What is unknown is whether the creature still stalks the Polish countryside to this day.

O Lobisón: South America's Werewolf

Over the past year, I've been in correspondence with a Brazilian researcher named Carlos Henrique Marquez. He informed me that South America is also home to its very own version of the werewolf, *o Lobisón*, and that he has personally interviewed several people who allege to have encountered these monsters. In its human form, this shape-shifter is reputed to display excessively yellow skin in addition to thick, calloused pads on its elbows and knees. One can supposedly identify one by the threads of victims' shredded clothing imbedded between its teeth. An elderly witness named Jandira claims to have encountered a Lobisón some fifty years ago and still maintains a vivid recollection of the incident.

According to Marquez, the encounter occurred in a rural area of northeastern Brazil while Jandira was standing in the kitchen of her ranch house one bright, moonlit evening. Glancing out the window, she noticed a strange man strolling up beside her horse stable. As she watched inquisitively, the stranger entered the *curral* (corral) and fell to the ground, rolling around in a pile of equine scat. After about a half an hour, Jandira, who was understandably hesitant to leave the safety of her kitchen, watched in utter disbelief as a horrible, man-sized dog rose ominously from the very spot where the man had been rolling about. The most terrifying detail, though, was the fact that the canine apparition was standing comfortably upright on its hind legs, like a man would. Within moments, the monstrous being vanished from Jandira's sight.

Another chilling and much more recent encounter stems from São Sepé, Rio Grande do Sul, and involves a twenty-year-old woman named Kelly Martins Becker. According to a filed police report, Becker claimed that she was scratched on the face and arms on January 28, 2009, by an animal that resembled a large dog but was walking exclusively on its hind legs. The victim's injuries were confirmed during a subsequent medical examination while incredulous detectives pursued the possibility that her attacker was someone sporting a werewolf costume. Six months earlier, residents from the rural area of Tauá, Ceará, had described run-ins with a "half man, half wolf" that was fond of breaking into houses as well as stealing sheep. Law enforcement officers were at a loss to explain the reports and dismissed it as a case of costume-wearing hooligans.

A quick search on the Internet will produce several videos that purport to show some of these Lobisones lurking in the shadowy streets of South American villages at night. While most of these clips seem to reek of dubious fraud (i.e., people in costumes), it is worth restating that legends are frequently born from some tiny grain of truth. And while I'm not necessarily disposed to endorsing the possibility of supernatural monsters per se, there are two factors worth considering here: werewolf lore is global, dating back centuries, and South America is a continent that seems to present an inordinate amount of both vastly weird accounts and new animal discoveries.

Black Panthers

If the notion of real-life werewolves ravaging the countryside seems a little hard to digest, there exist accounts of a different type of mystery predator that may have some real merit. Throughout both the United Kingdom and the United States there has been a multitude of alleged encounters with very large, jet-black felids (i.e., "panthers," which is a generic name for big cats) prowling along rural roadsides and eviscerating helpless livestock. The only problem is there are no known native feline species that adequately match the descriptions.

The largest plausible species of wildcat in the United Kingdom is the Eurasian lynx, a brown- or beige-colored animal that frequently displays spots and rarely reaches weights of over sixty pounds. Lynx are easily recognizable by their stubby tails, large feet, high hips, and trademark fur tufts sprouting from the apex of their pointy ears. Meanwhile, in North America the most sizable native cat is the so-called cougar or mountain lion (*Puma concolor*), which can occasionally grow to an impressive weight of some 230 pounds. Officially, cougars have been declared extinct in the eastern United States (except for a small population in southern Florida) but are fairly widespread throughout the rest of the Americas, and they are very nomadic and resilient animals. As recently as 2011, a rogue mountain lion was struck by a car in Milford, Connecticut. DNA tests revealed that the animal had wandered all the way from South Dakota, about 1,700 miles away. These mightily muscled cats always exhibit a tawny, tan, or light reddish-brown color. There has never been a confirmed instance of a melanistic (black) puma.

In fact, the only truly big cats that carry the gene that causes melanism are the leopard (*Panthera pardus*) of Asia and Africa, as well as a small percentage of jaguars (*Panthera onca*) found in South and Central America. So, ultimately, the claims of black panthers roaming Europe and North America are problematic.

Quite recently, a man named John wrote me the following letter, indicative of the many North American accounts:

> I grew up in Augusta, Georgia. In the early 1960s we took a field trip to the forest ranger tower deep in the woods, probably twenty to twenty-five miles outside of Augusta. When we got there, there was a dead black panther/cougar on the ground that the forest ranger had killed that morning. I remember being upset that he had killed it for no reason. I don't know if they still exist, but I've seen one dead five feet in front of me...I wish I could remember another person who was there. The troop leader and ranger are long deceased.

If only the pelt of this unique animal had been preserved, we might have been able to close the book on the black panther mystery long ago.

Carrabelle Cat

During the early part of 2012, I had an opportunity to travel to Florida's panhandle in order to investigate sightings of a baffling black panther known locally as the Carrabelle Cat. The expedition was organized by my friend and fellow cryptozoologist Scott Marlowe, an academic and long-time pursuer of mysterious creatures throughout Florida. I extended an invitation to naturalist Lee Hales, with whom I have collaborated on countless other projects. Hales is a close acquaintance with extensive experience tracking and studying a variety of fauna throughout North America. Our party had in fact received an official request from the Carrabelle city council to investigate, a very rare endorsement of such an endeavor by a US government entity.

Hales and I joined Marlowe in Panama City, Florida, at an exotic cat sanctuary known as the Bear Creek Feline Center. Run by a colorful man named Jim Broaddus, the facility houses an impressive collection of species, including African servals, lynx, jaguarundis, a stout Colorado mountain lion, and even some Florida panthers. The plan was to familiarize ourselves with the appearance and behavior of pumas and jaguarundis specifically, as both have been suggested as potential explanations for the Carrabelle Cat. It's been established that the accepted range of the puma is restricted to the southern portion of Florida, and jaguarundis (odd-looking, medium-sized, weasel-like cats with small craniums and long, bushy tails) are not officially native to the United States outside of extreme southern Texas. Experienced mystery cat researchers including Marlowe, Broaddus, and Chester Moore Jr. (a respected wildlife journalist) all feel that there could be a population of feral jaguarundis roaming the southeastern United States.

During our visit, Broaddus and his staff were extremely accommodating to say the least. Broaddus came across as a man who was exceptionally passionate about big cat conservation. He was even gracious enough to allow us to collect some

puma droppings and urine samples to aid us in our investigation. We planned on using it as an enticement, hopefully lur-
ing our quarry out of hiding and into the open.

A meandering, two-hour drive east from Panama City along
Florida's Gulf Coast lies Carrabelle, a small town nestled in the
appropriately named Tate's Hell State Forest, which is composed
of about 200,000 acres of highly foreboding wilderness area. It is
from here that accounts of black panthers have been surfacing
periodically, and one local hunter had supposedly even videotaped a mysterious, ebony feline that he felt was much larger
than anything native to that area. We planned to re-create the
scene from the footage on our trip and address its legitimacy.
Upon our team's arrival at a local diner, we met up with some of
the town's council members in order to discuss our expedition.

In the end, the better part of our excursion was impeded
by a steady deluge of heavy rain and at one point it even felt as
though our entire campsite might be washed out into the Gulf
of Mexico. Any fleeting respites were spent driving and hiking the back roads and trails of Tate's Hell State Forest while
surveying the surrounding habitat, searching for spoor. On
more than one occasion we stumbled upon what we identified
as black bear (*Ursus americanus floridanus*) droppings, proving that there is at least one species of large carnivore present
there, but we found no evidence of big cats in the area.

On the second to final day of our sojourn, the hunter who
had shot the video of the mystery cat led us to the exact spot
where he had filmed the animal. Using a full-sized cardboard
black panther model that we had fabricated, Hales and I attempted to recreate the incident. Hales climbed into the tree
where the hunter's deer stand had been positioned at the time

of the encounter, while I placed our model in the precise spot where the cat had been standing. Although the surrounding foliage had grown considerably in the two years since the footage had been shot, we were able to identify several large trees as landmarks. Hales took a series of photographs of our panther model for later comparison. Before leaving the spot, we created a feline "scratch pile" capped with our puma excreta and also set up a motion-activated surveillance camera to leave overnight.

We retrieved our camera trap the following morning, but, alas, the only animal we managed to photograph was the hunter's free-ranging dog sniffing and ultimately consuming most of our puma droppings. Upon reviewing our photographic recreation, the cat in the hunter's video did not look nearly as impressive as our cardboard cutout when the images were placed side by side. Digital analysis provided by a professional surveyor confirmed that the felid the hunter had videotaped was only fourteen inches tall at the shoulders and basically the size of a black house cat, a suspicion we had all harbored when we had initially observed its behavior and the erect posturing of its tail. And while we were ultimately able to reach a reasonable explanation for that particular red herring, we departed Carrabelle feeling that the potential was certainly still there for Tate's Hell to harbor an elusive, rarely seen predator.

While it seems likely that a considerable percentage of black panther reports can be attributed to fleeting glimpses of outsized domestic cats, it's difficult to explain them all away so easily. Marlowe is convinced that there is a melanistic morph of the Florida panther and is positive that he has seen one with his very own eyes. Researcher Chester Moore Jr. feels that some witnesses may be seeing black morph jaguarundis, while there may also be some black jaguars entering the United States via Mexico. Cryptozoologist Karl P.N. Shuker has another theory, suggesting that escaped or released black leopards are the culprits—apparently these Old World cats are a popular choice among exotic animal collectors. Regardless of their identity, black panthers seem to be among the most reported mystery beasts in the Western Hemisphere.

El Paso's Phantom Feline

It is known that small numbers of both jaguars and jaguarundis are occasionally creeping across the Mexican border into the southernmost parts of the United States, but what about a feline species that has never been documented before? A woman named Lydia wrote this to me about an intriguing encounter that she had near El Paso, Texas, in 1964:

> I was ten years old and walking my German shepherd dog on my usual route through my elementary school on a Saturday in broad daylight. We rounded a corner and there was a gigantic black feline. I have owned and loved cats all of my life and know a normal cat when I see one, and this was not. These days, I label it a cryptid. It was crouched with its bottom in the air. It was enormously muscled with a short Manx cat tail. It had gigantic strong hindquarters with extraordinarily long hind feet. Its short, pitch-black fur gleamed with health. Its eyes were literally the size of tea saucers, round, golden and calm. I, who know cats extremely well, would call it an amused stare. Not a feline expression that I had ever seen until then or since.... It did not seem to be quite as

long or as tall as my dog Max. It was crouching, so hard to tell. But I believe it weighed every bit as much as Max in sheer muscle mass (maybe 80 pounds).

Lydia recalls how, after a few seconds "transfixed," her dog instinctively turned away and coolly led her in the opposite direction, back toward their home. Halfway up the block, she glanced back and noticed that the creature had followed them to the very edge of the schoolyard, where it was still in a crouched position, intently staring at them in a menacing fashion. In retrospect, Lydia feels that Max may have saved both of their lives with his decisive action. "I never saw it move, but I know it must have been tracking behind us the whole way home—and I know it could have easily caught us.... That feline could have taken both of us."

Lydia then summarizes, "To preempt the usual [questions]: No, it was not an overgrown domestic Manx, a mountain lion, a bobcat, a lynx, or any other wild feline species. There are no pictures of that cat anywhere and never have been, because I have looked for years."

While I am inclined to wonder if Lydia and her pooch might have merely run across an exceptionally large bobcat, I have some reservations. Black bobcats, while exceedingly rare, do exist, and bobcats are prevalent in West Texas. But even the largest bobcats do not approach eighty pounds, unless Lydia was mistaken in her size estimate. Or, perhaps we're talking about a uniquely monstrous specimen here. Cryptid cat authority Karl P.N. Shuker has pointed out that the very same gene that causes melanism in felids also tends to make them grow larger than normal.

Mexican Marauder

During March of 2014, I was invited down to Mexico in order to participate in a television series on the Science Channel titled *Unexplained Files*. The topic of that particular episode was a string of baffling livestock killings that had occurred in the south central state of Puebla during 2010. According to local newspaper reports of the time, as many as 300 goats had been slaughtered in a matter of some fifty days by an unseen predator. At least fifty of the animals had been virtually decapitated. It wasn't long before the mythic, vampire-like *Chupacabra* (goat sucker) was proposed as the transgressor, due to the fact that whatever had eviscerated the goats had allegedly left scores of blood-drained carcasses in its wake. The Chupacabra legend needs little elaboration. Most readers by now are familiar with this legendary vampire, which has been grabbing headlines since the 1990s. However, in the course of pursuing my investigation it became palatable to conclude that the goats had in fact been the victims of a known varmint behaving in a totally unexpected manner and that accounts of the predation method had been grossly exaggerated.

Scouring the Internet, I'd initially been introduced to a startling image of about fifty dead goats that seemingly had their throats slit with surgical precision, seemingly too methodical to suggest any animal other than a human had been involved. Yet during production of the show, I was presented with a series of photographs of goats that displayed a range of gruesome injuries all over their bodies including deep, puncture wounds as well as long, sharp gashes that in some cases were causing large flaps of skin to drape open. These photos had been taken by ranchers whom I later had a chance to interview on camera. Strangely, these men described seeing only deep puncture wounds present in the throat region and a lack of blood that seemed to contradict the very photos they had taken. The goats in their care had obviously been attacked primarily from above by something that possessed razor-edged claws, long fangs, and evidently little interest in actually eating them. The disturbing detail was the fact that as many as eighty of the animals had been attacked in one bloodthirsty evening. Another ranch in the area had experienced a nearly identical slaughter around that same time period, but no photos had been taken of the victims in that particular incident.

In both instances, the livestock owners were at a total loss to explain what kind of predator could have made its way in over their tall fences, killing scores of animals in one evening and then disappearing quietly into the night without revealing its identity. However, I am convinced that the answer can be found by examining the most widespread and adaptable carnivore in the Americas, the mountain lion (*Puma concolor*).

While such cases are rare, there are documented occasions on which these powerful predators embarked on killing sprees that have resulted in dozens of sheep or goats being slaughtered in one singular event. These "thrill kills" have very little to do with the acquisition of sustenance and can best be explained as the result of a playful instinct that teeters on the edge of psychotic behavior. It's like when a house cat bats a poor rodent or lizard into submission and then leaves its pulverized body on the carpet, uneaten. It is precisely this type of bloodlust behavior but multiplied exponentially. Imagine the type of panic that might have ensued within a crowded goat pen if a mountain

lion had found its way in. The frenzied bleating and retreat-
ing of flocking goats would no doubt produce an adrenaline-
heightening effect on an animal whose killing instincts were
already approaching full throttle. Because such mass slaughters
are exceedingly rare, it's not impossible to imagine that the rural
ranchers, belonging to a relatively superstitious culture, might
suspect a supernatural culprit for the killings or other highly
unusual occurrences.

To underscore this point, during filming I was shown a
grotesque-looking specimen in a large glass jar that was presented to me as representing a deceased juvenile Chupacabra.
Villagers in the western state of Nayarit had come upon the small
carcass around the same time period in which farm animals and
even some local children had gone missing. The natives were
convinced that this monstrosity had somehow been connected
to the disappearances and had turned its remains over to the
local priest for safekeeping. Upon examining the cadaver, it became apparent to me that it was more likely a deformed, stillborn goat sporting extra limbs and a malformed skull. Despite
the fact that a forensic veterinarian at the local university verified my conclusion on camera, the priest remained loyal to the
belief of the village, insisting instead that the abomination was
undeniably a Chupacabra. It would appear that in many rural
locales, superstition still eclipses science.

An alleged juvenile Mexican Chupacabra preserved in a jar.

Chapter 4
SEA MONSTERS

Long before man was capable of traversing the globe simply by hopping onto an airplane, fearless sailors would embark on long journeys across the great, vast oceans. Upon returning to their home ports, such men often regaled others with stories of fabulous encounters with foreboding sea monsters capable of devouring entire vessels in one gulp. These creatures took a number of fantastic forms, including mermaids, sea bishops, and island-sized fish, as well as the insidious, multiarmed Kraken, thought to be inspired by the giant squid (*Architeuthis dux*), a cryptid in its own right for much of history. Yet ultimately no other mythical maritime beast has attained as lofty a status as the great Sea Serpent.

Olaus Magnus, a Swedish historian and writer, first mentioned a Norwegian serpent in the year 1555. He described the colossal creature as stretching some 200 feet in length and referred to it as the "Sea Orm" (Sea Worm). The thing had apparently been sighted off the coast of Norway for as long as anyone could remember. Around 200 years later, Erik Pontoppidan, a bishop of Bergen, also wrote about various sea monsters sighted off Norway's coast, including the Kraken and a titanic, black serpent that appeared during foreboding weather.

Hans Egede, the Apostle of Greenland, sighted a "terrible sea monster" while sailing the southwest coast of that island on July 6, 1734. He described the animal as being about one hundred feet in length and possessing a serpentine form, long pointed snout, and two enormous flippers. Egede noted that the subject's skin looked rough and mottled.

The creature spouted water like a whale when it broke the surface, and at one point its head appeared to be as high up in the air as the ship's masthead. One could hardly hope for a more credible witness than the pious Egede, who wrote about his other travels in a rather unsensational manner.

Stronsa Island, off the northern coast of Scotland, was the location of a strange find on September 25, 1808. Following a violent storm, the remains of a massive rotting beast washed up on the shore. Its body was described as being fifty-five feet long with three pairs of flippers attached. At the time, the Stronsa Beast created quite a stir in the scientific community, although later analysis of some of its preserved vertebrae indicated that the creature was most likely a decomposing basking shark (*Cetorhinus maximus*), albeit a monster-sized one. Still, the incident added fuel to the Sea Serpent debate.

During August of 1817, hundreds of Massachusetts residents reported watching a monstrous, serpent-like critter regularly frolicking in Gloucester Harbor. A special scientific committee was formed to investigate the sightings by interviewing the key eyewitnesses and then encouraging them to sign sworn affidavits describing their observations. At one point, a malformed snake that was found on an adjacent beach was declared to be the Sea Serpent's offspring. Despite that inopportune gaffe, there is little doubt that many reputable citizens saw something remarkable that summer.

While sailing off the southwest coast of Africa on August 6, 1848, Captain Peter McQuhae, Lieutenant Edgar Drummond, and at least five other officers and crewmembers aboard the HMS *Daedalus* spotted an unknown, sixty-foot-long animal swimming by their ship with a purpose. All got a good look at the creature and decided that its head, which was always held four feet above the water, most resembled that of an enormous snake. The beast seemed to display some type of mane or frill, or else something resembling a clump of seaweed washed about its back. This controversial incident received quite a bit of notoriety at the time and remains one of the most celebrated cases on record due to the veracity of many experienced observers who studied the thing at close proximity for twenty minutes. Various suggestions of misidentification were put forward; for example, perhaps what Captain McQuhae and his crew had seen was merely a long strand of seaweed. The eminent naturalist Sir Richard Owen became convinced that the incident involved a wayward seal that was seen out of context. Yet McQuhae and Drummond remained unwavering in their belief that the thing had been a genuine unknown.

On December 7, 1905, two trained zoologists, Edmund Meade-Waldo and Michael Nicoll, aboard the HMS *Valhalla* beheld an immense, unclassified serpentine animal while conducting a scientific expedition just off the coast of Brazil. Initially, its huge sail or frill breaking the surface of the water startled the men. They characterized the specimen as being brownish in color and light-colored underneath with an undersized, turtle-like head attached to a long neck that protruded about six feet out of the water. This may be the most compelling Sea Serpent report on record, due to the scientific credentials of the eyewitnesses involved. Considering all of these and thousands more accounts on record (potentially only scratching the surface), there seems to be little doubt that people have been observing some huge, unclassified sea animal for centuries. But what?

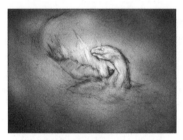

Meg Buick's interpretation
of the Valhalla Sea Serpent.

It goes without saying that there are considerable difficulties when dealing with a mystery that lives under the water, since the only sighted features are those that briefly breach the surface when the thing resolves to make a rare appearance. Yet when analyzing and comparing thousands of documented descriptions of Sea Serpents (and also seemingly related lake monsters) around the world, a remarkably consistent model emerges. The general archetype is of an elongate animal averaging at least thirty feet in length (though much greater lengths have been reported), possessing a dark-colored, smooth (not scaly) hide; a lengthy neck that protrudes about five or six feet out of the water; and a small head that resembles that of a sheep, cow, or horse. Descriptions of the head that draw comparisons to turtles or snakes may have more to do with perception of the observers, particularly if they don't see protruding ears. Other frequently mentioned features include large eyes, sets of flippers, and in some cases facial whiskers, bristly hair around the neck, or even horns. Many eyewitnesses remark on the creature's vertically undulating humps or coils that break the surface of the water, making its back appear extremely flexible. This feature may account for the Norwegian legends that refer to them as *orms* (worms).

Presently there is nothing known, either extant or even in the fossil record, which perfectly corresponds to all of these characteristics, particularly when one notes the Sea Serpent's alleged habit of extending its small head and swan-like neck straight out of the water like a periscope. It is true that millions of years ago the planet's waterways were teaming with massive, aquatic reptiles, some of which (the plesiosaurs) had exceptionally long necks supporting their relatively small heads. However, these species also possessed rigid, thickset bodies unlikely to create the humps and vertical undulations described with regard to our Sea Serpents. Besides, the notion of either a true serpent or any cold-blooded reptile for that matter (archaic or otherwise) thriving in the icy waters where sea monsters have been encountered is problematic in terms of survival, though there has been recent speculation that plesiosaurs may in fact have been warm-blooded like mammals and birds.

As far back as 1896, the Dutch biologist Anthonie Cornelis (A. C.) Oudemans suggested a mammalian identity for the long-necked mystery animals mistakenly called "Sea Serpents," specifically a heretofore undocumented species of long-necked pinniped (the suborder that includes seals, sea lions, and walruses). The father of cryptozoology, Bernard Heuvelmans, endorsed this possibility as well. During 2012, I received a report that may add some weight to this theory.

Nova Scotia resident and author Jenny Tyson related the following experience to me. An extended telephone interview with her reinforced my opinion that she was extremely credible, given her familiarity with marine mammals and the ocean, and in position to judge that the exceptional specimen she observed was doubtless something out of the ordinary.

I saw the creature a couple of years ago, shortly after we moved to Cape Breton. I've lived on the coast here for several years. In Maine (Vinalhaven Island), we had seals in both coves near the house, so I'm used to being around them. I've also seen pilot whales and harbor porpoises in the wild. I went to the beach below the lighthouse on Point Aconi. The area can only be safely accessed when hiking along the shore at a dropping or low tide. This was after one of the early fall storms. Seas outside were rough, temperature about 0° Celsius, and winds about seventy kilometers per hour with higher gusts. These weather conditions almost always prevail after a big storm. I enjoy watching the storms leave, and the sight is usually spectacular, especially in the fall and early winter before the snow sets in.

I settled before the base of the cliffs where the lighthouse stands in order to watch the waves. I saw what I thought was initially a pilot whale beaching on the rocks very close about fifteen to twenty feet away. The animal turned over and raised its head, and I saw it was a seal. It spotted me, barked, and then scooted off towards deeper water. It wasn't scared of me and wasn't in a hurry. The size of the animal was nearly triple that of any seal I've ever seen before. Probably around twenty feet, and that is a conservative estimate. The body color was identical to a pilot whale—kind of a dark grey with a fair bit of brown in it. The head was identical to a harbor seal, only much larger. It was smooth; no bulges like an elephant seal has. Nor did it have the slimmer neck of a sea lion. Front flippers were also the same as a harbor seal, only much longer.

Although Tyson's monster seal did not display the elongate neck of Oudemans's theoretical "serpent" seal, its dimensions if accurate are staggering. Harbor seals only grow to an accepted length of about six feet or so, and while the largest known species of elephant seal can obtain lengths up to twenty-two feet, they are not native to the North Atlantic. Besides, bull elephant seals display a prominent proboscis that is unmistakable, hence their name. If Tyson's estimate of size is correct, the prospect of finding immense, undocumented pinnipeds in the Earth's oceans is worth considering.

A Whale of a Theory

Even the most conservative scientists will acknowledge that there are sizable species living deep in the Earth's oceans that remain undocumented. Still, these same academics have not yet been provided the tangible proof they require in order to proclaim the Sea Serpent a reality. All of the evidence for these aquatic monsters is anecdotal—scores of eyewitness accounts and legends spanning centuries, inconclusive photos, and sonar anomalies. As of yet, no one has been able to produce a physical specimen or even a tooth or bone. However, it's worth noting that a considerable number of vivid encounters have been logged by mariners and fishermen, people who are intimately familiar with a vast assortment of sea life. Could they all be mistaken?

The prevalent theories about Sea Serpents suggest surviving marine reptiles left over from the Cretaceous Period, monster-sized eels, or a species of heretofore undiscovered long-necked pinniped. I tend to agree with the late cryptozoologist Roy Mackal that the most likely candidates to explain the Sea Serpent or lake monster enigma might be surviving representatives of the archaeocetes, a suborder of ancient whales that first appeared during the Eocene epoch some fifty-five million years ago and presumably died out twenty-five million years ago during the Miocene. In particular, one exceptionally snake-like genus known as *Basilosaurus* is intriguing and a strong contender for a number of reasons.

- Sea Serpents are always described as displaying a vertical undulating motion when moving through the water, typically a mammalian trait.

- They have frequently been characterized as having smooth, whalelike skin and heads that resemble mammals such as horses or sheep and as sometimes displaying manes or whiskers, and some witnesses have even described bilobate, horizontal tails. These physical attributes, along with a serpentine body shape, could conceivably correspond with how *Basilosaurus* actually looked.

• The reported lengths of sixty to one hundred feet fall perfectly in line with the largest marine animals, the cetaceans (whales and dolphins).

• As warm-blooded animals, they would be well acclimated, even comfortable, in the very frigid water temperatures of the North Atlantic as well as the glacial "monster" lakes such as Loch Ness (the habitat of Nessie), New York's Lake Champlain (Champ) and Canada's Okanagan Lake (Ogopogo). Cetaceans have been known to occasionally stray into freshwater rivers and lakes, and there are even species of dolphins that have adapted exclusively to those conditions.

• There have been observations, including that of Egede, of these animals spouting water, as whales are known to do.

• Some of the most rarely encountered marine animals are the beaked whales, which live at great depths. Multiple new species of cetaceans have been catalogued in recent decades, and there is little doubt that other species await discovery.

The suggestion that our so-called Sea "Serpents" may actually be snakelike whales is not a new one. As early as 1860, naturalist Philip Henry Gosse advocated this possibility. Really the only feature that becomes problematic when relating the accounts to cetacean physiology is the strikingly elongate neck that is described. I can only speculate that this could be a specialized adaptation that represents an example of convergent evolution. After all, the plesiosaurs flourished in the Earth's oceans for many millions of years with just such a design. By nature of their slender form, the basilosaurs had a head start in this direction already. Who's to say their descendants' neck vertebrae could not have gradually lengthened over the past 30 million years or so as they carved out a new niche? The fossil evidence is lacking, but the possibility is worth considering. Admittedly, we need proof rather than speculation.

Raystown Ray

During December of 2012, I was invited to participate in an investigation of a monster that has been periodically reported in Pennsylvania's Raystown Lake. The mysterious beast, which has been depicted as a serpentine animal extending some fifteen feet in length, has been assigned the very obvious nickname "Ray" and is purportedly quite distinct from the multitude of endemic fish found in the lake, including striped bass, trout, catfish, and Atlantic salmon. The lake itself is a manmade reservoir that only achieved its current depth and dimensions as recently as 1973, when construction of a dam was completed. It is as deep as two hundred feet in some places. The meandering Juniata and Susquehanna Rivers connect Raystown Lake to the Atlantic Ocean, and it is the largest lake wholly contained within the state of Pennsylvania.

My partners on this particular expedition included Bill Hoolahan, a seasoned skipper and scuba expert whose passion is hunting for sunken ships and lost treasure; Phil Abernathy, a cryptozoology enthusiast, fossil collector, and experienced fisherman; and Dr. Cheska Burleson, a marine biologist. We had been brought together by an anonymous benefactor who had an interest in seeing how such pursuits might be under-taken on a regular basis.

Our initial meeting with a local historian revealed that the fleeting descriptions of Ray were fairly consistent—essentially, it was a large, snakelike creature, and its first appearance corre-sponded with the alleged crash of a circus train decades earlier. If this explanation sounds uncomfortably familiar, it should. One of the most prevalent urban legends around the United States speaks of circus train accidents, the results of which have been all manner of unusual and exotic beasts roaming the countryside. Nonetheless, our contact was adamant that the locals had been observing and also photographing some-thing genuinely mysterious in Raystown Lake for decades.

Our suspicions were aroused when we visited the local re-sort's gift shop, where we found ourselves surrounded by a healthy supply of Raystown Ray T-shirts, bumper stickers, post cards, and coffee mugs. It was evident that the community was eager to embrace their very own monster if it could help stimu-late the local economy. The iconic image of Ray plastered ev-erywhere was based on a photograph that had been allegedly taken by a fisherman during 2006, as the monster supposedly surfaced across from a local marina. The image seemed to pos-sess a surreal quality that I couldn't quite ignore. When we were shown what was described to us as a cast of one of Ray's three-toed footprints (apparently made after the animal had wan-dered onto the shore), I questioned why the plaster mold was a negative impression, as opposed to a three dimensional cast that one might expect to produce when pouring plaster into nega-tive space. The woman behind the counter merely shrugged her shoulders. The description of a serpentine animal had taken a weird turn: it now possessed dinosaur feet.

Despite our misgivings about the void of compelling evidence for old Ray, our team spent the next couple of days out on the lake, primarily utilizing a fish-finding sonar unit that we had brought along in order to scan the depths for unusually large objects. We also decided to stack the deck in our favor by chumming the water around our boat, in hopes of drawing in more fish as well as anything else that might potentially live in the lake. An underwater camera I had brought along was not functioning as I had hoped, but Captain Hoolahan used the opportunity to attempt some scuba diving in the lake's frigid, murky water.

In spite of our team's combined efforts, our investigation came up empty, which is hardly a surprising result considering the great difficulties involved in lake-monster research. Consider that Raystown Lake is twenty-eight miles long (essentially 8,300 acres). That is a lot of ground to cover when the object of your pursuit is obscured below you in the great, cloudy depths and is probably on the move to boot.

If there are sizeable unknown animals living in the lakes of the world, they are seemingly quite rare and elusive, perhaps spending the majority of their time in the boundless oceans and only visiting freshwater lakes via connecting river systems on fleeting occasions. The similarities in descriptions between lake monsters and Sea Serpents are so analogous that there can be little doubt we are talking about the very same animal. If they are not tragically teetering on the edge of extinction like so many species in the world's waterways, perhaps we will be fortunate enough to find them one day.

Raystown Lake, Pennsylvania,
is rumored to be home to a lake monster.

Fantastic Fish of the Far North

Lake Iliamna is the largest lake in the great state of Alaska as well as the second biggest freshwater body contained wholly in the United States and one of the largest worldwide. It is often referred to as an inland sea. Its dimensions are seventy-seven miles long by twenty-two miles wide with an area of roughly 1,000 square miles and an average depth of 144 feet, though there are trenches that may go down 1,000 feet or more. Sparsely populated along the shore and accessible to humans by boat or floatplane only, it claims some sizeable inhabitants, including an unusual population of freshwater seals and, on occasion, scant numbers of beluga whales and orcas that travel from the ocean up the Kvichak River. According to native legends and numerous modern sightings, there may also be another resident, monstrous and highly aggressive, that has defied discovery up to this point. Known to the indigenous people of the area as *Jig-ik-nak* and to other Alaskans as Illie, (short for Iliamna, of course) the piscine animal is said to be a titanic fish possessing a length of anywhere from ten to thirty feet.

Now, if we were talking about salt water, some prolific, pelagic fish would immediately spring to mind. But when it comes to freshwater lakes and rivers, the issue becomes vastly more complicated, since nonsaline species typically do not get too huge. As you might expect, Iliamna boasts a fairly healthy and diverse population of fish. Trophy salmon, trout, and northern pike abound. Still, the record sizes of all those species top out at about six feet in length and around fifty pounds in weight, nowhere near the sizes that are described for Illie.

Tales of the creature date back to before the colonization of the Americas. One dramatic story tells of a group of Aleut who were scouring one of the lake's southernmost rock islands for seagull eggs when, suddenly, an unseen "something" capsized one of their *bidarka* (kayaks), causing a man to sink below the depths and disappear, presumably eaten. It is said that the victim violated one of the cardinal rules by staring down into the water, thus invoking the wrath of the monster. Regardless, the incident frightened his tribe so badly that they refused to go out on the lake for weeks afterwards. On the eastern end, the Kenaitze Indians have always viewed the monster as a bad omen. Small children are warned not to go too close to the water or else the beast will drown them, and it is believed that to see the creature inevitably leads to shriveling up and dying. A prevalent superstition states that Jig-ik-nak despises the color red, so early travelers on the lake were careful not to paint their vessels that color. Caribou swimming across the lake are at risk of being devoured, or so the legend states.

Today, the number of alleged sightings leaves little doubt that remarkable animals inhabit the lake. Beginning in the fall of 1941, a local game warden by the name of Carlos Carson was flying over the mouth of Talarik Creek in a floatplane and spotted a number of "logs," which quickly sank from sight. His passenger later stated, "We spotted the huge mystery fish, about ten or twelve of them near a small island off the shore of what is known as Big Mountain. At the time we spotted the fish, we were cruising at an altitude of around 1,000 feet, and as we turned and slowed our aircraft down to get a better look, the big fish seemed to sink slowly into the deep water, but not before we had several looks at them."

The most celebrated encounter occurred the following year and involved well-known bush pilot and guide Babe Aylesworth as well as his passenger, a colorful local fisherman named Bill Hammersley. Traveling from Naknek to Anchorage in a Stinson ferry plane, they were gliding at an altitude of 1,000 feet over a twenty-five mile stretch of Iliamna on a bright, clear day. The lake was flat and calm, and visibility into the deep blue water was exceptional. As they approached a horseshoe-shaped island associated with the monsters, Aylesworth excitedly shouted, "My God! What big fish!" Looking down, Hammersley saw what his companion was referring to—dozens of them just below the surface in the shallows, dull aluminum in color, with broad and blunt heads, long tapering bodies, and vertical tail fins that were swaying back and forth.

Aylesworth's initial size estimate of a few feet proved to be way off once he circled around and reduced his altitude to around 300 feet. The fish were at least ten feet long in Hammersley's opinion but perhaps twice that length, since they seemed comparable to the pontoons of the plane. They looked to weigh at least 300 pounds. After about twenty minutes of being observed by the men, the fish turned and swam away from the island, submerging into deeper water and out of sight. The experienced outdoorsmen quickly discounted beluga whales, salmon, trout, and sturgeon as possible explanations. They were both in agreement that whatever they had seen could not be explained easily.

In 1947, Hammersley published an account of the incident in hopes of encouraging other witnesses to come forward. One who did was Larry Rost, a pilot for the US Coast and Geodetic Survey. Rost told Hammersley that he had flown over the exact same spot during the fall of 1945 and had seen a twenty-foot fish from an altitude of one hundred feet. The creature had displayed the same aluminum color that Aylesworth and Hammersly had noted.

Over the next decade and a half, several attempts were made to capture the monsters. In August of 1959, Texas oil millionaire and adventurer Tom Slick spent five days on the lake, accompanied by guide and lodge owner Bob Walker. The two men deployed heavy-duty shark tackle with no result. Slick offered a reward of $1,000 to anyone who could provide proof that the animals existed, inspiring three veteran sportsmen—Gil Paust, Slim Beck, and John Walatka—who devised a creative approach. The anglers attached a hundred feet of steel airplane cable to a one-foot iron hook, which was baited with the hindquarter of a moose. Their bobber was a five-gallon oil drum. The entire rig was attached to the pontoon of a large floatplane that they set down where Hammersley, Aylesworth, and Rost had all seen the mystery fish. That night something snapped the cable, taking a strut from the airplane down with it. The men had apparently obtained a permit to use dynamite too, but never had a chance to use it. Yet another fisherman baited a heavy line and tied it to a tree, but by the next morning the bait was gone and the tree had been uprooted.

Numerous sightings followed. In August of 1959, two helicopter pilots hovering over the same spot got a good look at four sharklike fish that were five to eight feet long. The very next year, a geologist and two companions in a plane observed four fish with an estimated length of about ten feet. During 1963, a biologist reported seeing a twenty-five- to thirty-foot animal from the air, and he was sure it wasn't a whale, since it never surfaced. This was followed by an organized search in 1966 that included Captain Lee from Kodiak Island as well as nature photographer Leonard Rue. Missionary Chuck Crapuchettes was the next person to witness the monster and on two different occasions, actually; once was from a floatplane in 1967. After a full decade had passed, air taxi pilot Tim LaPorte was flying over San Pedro Bay when he saw a twelve- to fourteen-foot fish just below the surface. In 1987, resident Verna Kolyaha and others observed a large, black fish that surfaced in front of them, revealing a stripe on its back. Two years later, boater Louise Wassille watched a twenty-foot fish that appeared to have a prominent snout. Finally, Tim LaPorte claimed yet another sighting at the turn of the century.

So then, what might the Lake Iliamna monsters truly represent? It seems safe to eliminate beluga whales as candidates, since they are not an uncommon sight in the lake and are in fact quite conspicuous with their pasty white coloration, not to mention that whales (being mammals) must frequently come up for air. For the popular television program *River Monsters,* host Jeremy Wade conducted an investigation and concluded that the creatures were most likely sturgeons, migratory fish that grow to substantial sizes in the ocean and then swim up rivers in order to spawn. North American white sturgeons (*Acipenser transmontanus*) are prehistoric-looking, armor-plated fish that have been known to reach lengths of eleven feet and live for over a century. The largest sturgeon on record was a European specimen (*Huso huso*) from Russia's Volga River (circa 1827) that was reportedly twenty-four feet in length and weighed 3,463 pounds. Because they are bottom-feeders, hypothetical monster sturgeons would rarely be seen, and the frigid water temperatures of Iliamna would ensure that they sink to the bottom when they died. The issue is that no sturgeon has ever been documented in Lake Iliamna, though small ones have apparently been caught in nearby Bristol Bay and Cook Inlet.

Another intriguing theory is that the Lake Iliamna monsters could be large sharks that traveled up the Kvichak River from the ocean. During 2012, a Pacific sleeper shark (*Somniosus pacificus*) was filmed splashing around in the brackish water of King Cove, Alaska, which lies in the Aleutian Islands. These cold-water sharks may be capable of exceeding lengths of twenty-three feet, according to scientist Bruce Wright, who speculates that the ocean dwellers may be capable of tolerating freshwater on occasion (by a process known as osmoregulation). Bull sharks (*Carcharhinus leucas*) have been known to swim up rivers for extended periods and are commonly reported in Lake Nicaragua in Central America. The Pacific sleeper shark does fit some of the descriptions of Illie nicely, possessing a dull brownish-gray coloration in addition to a blunt head. However, we can't discount the possibility that Lake Iliamna harbors a gigantic, new species of fish that has never been documented. Due to the lake's relative inaccessibility, immense size, and treacherous waves and currents, it may be a long time before the mystery is put to rest.

Boasting over 6,000 miles of coastline and three million lakes, Alaska can lay claim to many aquatic enigmas. In Inuit folklore, the *Tizheruk* or *Pal-Rai-Yuk* is a monstrous serpentine animal that lives in the ocean and regularly snatches unsuspecting victims from docks and vessels. To the Tlingit people, the *Gonakadet* is a sea monster that combines the characteristics of a wolf and killer whale. Chandler Lake in northern central Alaska is rumored to be home to trout that are four feet in length and to an unknown fish that is at least ten feet long, is dark on top with a reddish underside, and has very black eyes. Monster fish have also been reported in Crosswind Lake and Lake Minchumina, as well as Nonvianuk Lake and Walker Lake.

Back in November of 1930, two fox farmers discovered a massive carcass floating in Eagle Bay off Glacier Island. The two men towed the thing ashore but couldn't identify it. Word of the strange find quickly spread, and weeks later the oddity was featured in the *New York Sun*, which prompted a team of naturalists to launch an on-site investigation. The creature was said to be twenty-four feet long and to resemble a huge lizard with a long, flat skull, though parts of it seemed to be covered in hair or fur. Speculation at the time was that the animal most likely was some type of prehistoric beast that had been frozen in the nearby Columbia Glacier for thousands of years, until the ice in which it was entombed had broken off into the ocean. Ultimately, the specimen ended up at the National Museum of Natural History in Washington, DC, where it was determined to be the remains of a northern minke whale (*Balaenoptera acutorostrata*).

A similar incident occurred in July of 1956 when newspapers around the world announced that a colossal carcass had washed up on the shore of Dry Harbor, which lies sixty miles southeast of Yakutat. The object was said to be one hundred feet long, fifteen feet wide, and covered in reddish-brown hair that was two inches long. The skull was estimated to be five-and-a-half feet across, with large eye sockets and a protruding, tusk-like upper jaw lined with six-inch teeth. Scientists were understandably enthusiastic, since the description matched no known animal. However, a short time later a photo was published which showed a floatplane pilot named Loren Horn who had landed his craft next to the thing and posed with it. Anyone viewing the image instantly surmised that the initial accounts were grossly inaccurate, as the carcass appeared to be only a fraction of the size reported. Based on this revelation, a scientist named W. A. Clemons declared that the remains were that of a rare Baird's beaked whale (*Berardius bairdii*).

In recent years, a video purporting to show a pod of Sea Serpents off the coast of Alaska stirred up controversy in the field of cryptozoology. During 2009, local fisherman Kelly Nash, along with his two sons, sighted several large, marine animals swimming in Nushagak Bay in the far southwest part of the state. They began to videotape the creatures, which appeared to be swimming in a straight-line formation and fleeing a pod of beluga whales. Highly experienced at viewing all manner of sea critters, Kelly and the Nash boys were convinced that they were not observing whales, sea lions, or anything known. The things looked to be snakelike, about twenty feet long, and they had serrated backs. At times, the subjects appeared to lift their heads out of the water.

Consequently, the footage was reviewed by cryptid researchers Paul LeBlond and John Kirk of the British Columbia Scientific Cryptozoology Club. LeBlond is a former director of the Earth, Ocean, and Atmospheric Sciences Department at the University of British Columbia, and Kirk (a good friend and colleague of mine) has experience in law enforcement in addition to having worked at an oceanographic theme park in Hong Kong. Both men are regarded as two of the world's top investigators of mysterious sea creatures. Blogging on the website *Cryptomundo*, Kirk said that he was stunned when one of the animals seemed to raise its head out of the water and look directly at the camera, displaying a "cameloid" head and face identical to descriptions of Canada's famous Sea Serpent, Cadborosaurus. For him, this was definitive evidence that the video showed massive marine animals of a previously unclassified type.

Shortly thereafter, Nash sold the rights to the footage to a television production company for tens of thousands of dollars. Following a gap of two years, the film was finally made public as part of a television program titled *Alaskan Monster Hunt: Hillstranded,* which featured two stars from *Deadliest Catch,* a popular series about the Alaska fishing industry. Unfortunately, the show only presented a brief, inconclusive segment of the video and did not reveal the evidence that inspired LeBlond and Kirk's eureka moment. When John inquired about matter, he ran up against a wall: neither the Nash family nor the television network could provide answers to why the program did not include the definitive portion of the film or if it had even ever existed. Further digging by Kirk led him to a disheartening conclusion. Quite possibly someone had inadvertently lost or taped over the most compelling section of the footage, ensuring that an important piece of evidence would be lost forever. The field of cryptozoology seems to be cursed by comparable gaffes and near misses.

If strange, new animals remain to be found anywhere on our planet, our unexplored oceans and waterways seem to be the most likely place. Even the most conservative scientists agree that there are potentially sizeable aquatic organisms that we haven't seen yet. Three quarters of the Earth's surface is covered by this foreboding marine environment, which harbors an average depth of twelve thousand feet and includes some trenches that lie five miles down. The giant squid, megamouth shark, and beaked whale are a few of the recent discoveries that serve as important reminders. Yet the most remarkable example may be the coelacanth, an archaic fish that was dredged up off the coast of South Africa in 1938. Scientists already knew of the coelacanth from fossils that were millions of years old, but they assumed that it had gone extinct along with the dinosaurs. Perhaps other prehistoric survivors may dwell beneath the watery abyss.

The author is shown with a fossilized coelacanth,
an ancient fish that was discovered alive and well in 1938.

Chapter 5
ENORMOUS EAGLES

Over the course of decades, I have been gathering accounts of the enigmatic and suitably named Thunderbirds that are reportedly soaring throughout the skies of North America. A multitude of Native American cultures embraces legends that feature the massive Thunderbird as a central character and include the belief that the animal creates thunder by the beating of its mighty wings. The modern descriptions are remarkably consistent. Observers have portrayed these creatures as resembling immense, dark-colored raptors (birds of prey), with wingspans ranging anywhere from twelve to twenty-five feet across—approaching the width of a small airplane. Size estimates are significant because the largest scientifically recognized bird species all possess wingspreads that are less than a dozen feet. It follows that if these monster birds actually do exist, we are dealing with truly extraordinary animals.

The widest accepted wingspan belongs to the wandering albatross (*Diomedea exulans*), a highly nomadic and gracile sea bird that doesn't even begin to approximate what Thunderbird witnesses have described, though its impressive wings can extend almost a dozen feet across. Another example is Africa's marabou stork (*Leptoptilos crumeniferus*), also with unconfirmed wingspreads approaching a dozen feet. These long-legged, wading birds have long, straight bills and a two-toned body that features black wings attached to an ivory breast. The bulkiest North American birds, California condors (*Gymnogyps californianus*), are most reminiscent of what many have characterized and have a wingspan of around ten feet. But the species is endangered, with a closely monitored population of over 200 individuals inhabiting parts of California, Mexico, Arizona, and Utah. All of the sizable raptors in North America, such as eagles, have wingspans that only extend from seven to eight feet across, so the notion of a bird two or three times that size is a tall order indeed—at least in modern times.

Presently, we know from hundreds of fossil finds that truly wondrous birds did once exist in the Americas up until ten thousand years ago, at the end of the Pleistocene epoch. These creatures were known as the teratorns, and they were ostensibly the big, bad forerunners of present day condors and vultures, with a possible affiliation to the stork family as well. One archaic species (*Argentavis magnificens*) that was identified in Argentina during the 1970s boasted a wingspan approaching twenty-four feet and weighed as much as a man, though a substantial North American cousin (*Aiolornis incredibilis*) wasn't far behind with its eighteen-foot spread. While difficult to fathom, it is not wholly unthinkable that a relict population of these gigantic birds still lingers on some distant, craggy mountain peak.

Another possibility is that witnesses could be glimpsing an extant group of unknown eagles, perhaps akin to the controversial Washington's eagle, described by the great naturalist and painter John James Audubon in the early part of the nineteenth century. However, most modern ornithologists presume that Audubon was mistaken in his pronouncement that there was a tremendous but rare sea eagle endemic to North America, larger than any known species. A final option is that nature may infrequently generate grossly outsized individuals of the known eagle species and that these freak specimens are what people are observing from time to time. My colleague Richard Freeman refers to this peculiarity as the "Goliath gene." Quite possibly, this condition might equate to an atavism, essentially a throwback trait hailing from an age when animals grew to much greater statures.

The fundamental archetype of the contemporary Thunderbird somewhat corresponds with numerous Native American legends, which speak of enormous eagles so expansive that they are in some myths capable of eclipsing the sun when they soar overhead. The origin of the term "Thunderbird" may pay homage to the thunderous, booming sound of their beating wings, or perhaps it can be attributed to the fact that these heavy raptors exploit the thermals and updrafts of approaching storm fronts in order to stay aloft.

Most of my research has admittedly but justifiably been focused on my native state of Texas, as the region seems to produce a significant number of sightings. Other traditional hotbeds of activity include mountainous northern central Pennsylvania as well as the state of Illinois. It's unclear why this is the case, as these disparate regions do not necessarily harbor ecosystems that would be considered ideal for sustaining a population of giant raptors. And while the notion of discovering giant undocumented avians nesting in highly populated states such as Texas, Illinois, or Pennsylvania seems rather improbable to say the least, the odds are much better in the vast, remote mountain ranges of the West.

Meg Buick's interpretation of an enormous eagle.

Thunderbirds over Alaska

During October of 2002, there were two highly publicized incidents that took place in southwestern Alaska. On October 5, an experienced bush pilot named John Bouker (along with his passenger Nikolai Alakayak) spotted a "really, really big" bird flying about 500 yards away from Bouker's Cessna airplane as he descended into the community of Manokotak. Bouker described the bird as having a golden-brown hue and a hooked beak. He felt certain that the animal's wingspan equaled that of one of his vessel's wings, around fourteen feet or so. Just four days later, local tractor operator Moses Coupchiak saw presumably the same bird approaching the nearby village of Togiak. At first he had assumed that the object was an airplane until it flapped its mighty wings. Coupchiak was so concerned about the safety of the local children that he broadcast a warning over his shortwave radio.

Thunderbird tales are not new to Alaska. They date back generations. The native peoples immortalized these mythical beasts on the totem poles that pepper the Pacific Northwest. They were considered to be substantially more significant than common eagles by tribes who revered all animals, and they held these creatures in especially high regard. What's intriguing is that there has been consistent trickle of modern Thunderbird accounts dating back to the early 1970s. One Alaskan couple even alleged that they spotted a truly titanic bird over Noorvik in 1972 that they thought might be hunting for caribou. In recent years, I've heard from a handful of eyewitnesses from the great state of Alaska. A man named David shared the following story with me in 2011.

> I took my two sons last spring to a place called Tangle Lakes to fish for lake trout and camp out. The lakes are in open tundra mountains. Not many trees around the area. We decided to check one of the other lakes nearby. When we got to the lake we all saw a large bird that looked like a plane. It was so big. It swooped down to the middle of the lake and grabbed a big fish, then flew to the other side of the lake and landed. I jumped in my truck, drove around to the other side of the lake,

and watched him with binoculars. It ripped the fish to pieces and ate it. My boys and I never forgot that. It was amazing.

I was also contacted by Margaret from tiny Nenana, Alaska, who wrote this:

My late husband worked in Denali National Park the summers of 2004–2005. An outdoorsman all of his life, as well as being an excellent hunter and crack shot. He told me he sighted a very large bird perched upon the rocky crags where he often stopped to look for mountain goats. Being familiar with this particular site, he had a good concept of distance and size; at first the thought it was a human standing on the crags. He dragged out his binoculars and said he was shocked to see it was a bird, a very large bird. His estimate was a minimum of five feet from head to tail. He stated that it was dark brown in color, mottled to lighter, somewhat like a juvenile golden eagle but much larger than any eagle he'd ever seen. The bird had its back to him. When it flew, it just dropped over the other side of the crags, so he only got a short glimpse of the wingspan, which he said was huge... again, larger than any eagle he'd ever seen. Several other workers in Denali Park have also stated they have periodically seen this or another bird like it.

One final account from Alaska is worth reviewing as well. It comes from an individual named Carlos, who may have sighted an outsized bird in 1997.

I'm from Point Baker/Port Protection, Alaska, on Prince of Wales Island in one of the last and largest stands of old growth forest left anywhere in North America. About twelve years ago, I was walking to my friend's house on the boardwalk (no roads or cars, only a boardwalk through the woods), and I saw a huge bird flying through the forest canopy overhead. The coloring was a light shade of golden brown, and I would estimate the wingspan between fifteen and twenty feet. I known one of the difficulties of measuring a flying animal high overhead is that you have no sense of scale to take measurements, but this bird was within the forest canopy for the first five or six seconds that I saw it, and the spruce and hemlock trees in my hometown are usually between one and two hundred feet tall. It wasn't a golden eagle. For one, it was much too large and those birds aren't native to Prince of Wales Island. It wasn't an immature bald eagle either. The coloration was wrong. I mean, I've see bald eagles my entire life, and I'm pretty sure I know what they look like during the first three to five years of their lives, before they get the white heads and tails. Anyway, the bird took off through the canopy, up into the open sky and out of my line of vision. I watched it for a good thirty-five to forty seconds, though.

Quite recently, Carlos admitted to me that upon further reflection he could have been mistaken about the bird he saw, perhaps grossly overestimating its size. Regardless, if Thunderbirds do exist, one could hardly hope for a more promising habitat than the state of Alaska—a boundless wilderness teeming with abundant mountains, water, towering trees, and ample prey. Moving southeast to the equally encouraging Rocky Mountains, the reports continue.

Montana's Monster Birds

The state of Montana is commonly referred to as Big Sky Country. It is a majestic territory of stunning visual beauty and wide, open spaces. It also boasts a relatively tiny population relative to its vast land area. Perhaps it's safe to assume that where there are big skies, there are big birds compelled to fly across them, and this definitely seems to be the case in Montana.

The earliest sighting that I'm aware of dates back to October of 1987. A young man named Matthew O'Brien and his father were on a road trip heading east on Interstate 90, somewhere in the midsection of Montana, between the mountains and flatlands. Suddenly and without warning, a giant bird flew over. It was the largest bird that O'Brien had ever seen, with a wingspan around fifteen feet, or twice as big as an eagle or vulture. The encounter only lasted about fifteen seconds or so, and since they were traveling around sixty miles per hour with the animal positioned at least a few hundred feet above them, they only caught a brief glimpse of it, though it obviously made quite the impression. O'Brien stated to me that the subject was a bird of prey, and in his opinion it most resembled a California condor, despite the fact that they are not known to be indigenous there. But, as we have established, condors do not possess wingspans anywhere approaching fifteen feet.

The next incident occurred during early September of 1994, when a twenty-one-year-old named Tony was backpacking with his younger brother at a spot known as Beartooth Plateau, a high-elevation mountain range on the border of Wyoming. One night as they were camping alongside a small lake, they suddenly heard a loud splash, as if something heavy had been dropped into the water. Tony explained,

At this point something caught my eye in my upper peripheral vision, and it was moving fast. I reacted by spinning back around and looking up at the same time. What I saw doesn't fit into the reality I know. The entire sky full of stars was blacked out as something flew over me. It was a giant silhouette of a birdlike shape. ... I'm guessing at least ten feet above me but perhaps much more. If that's the case, then the size of it must have been enormous. Twenty-foot wingspan? Thirty feet? I don't know, but it was huge.

Within the past year, I also received an intriguing e-mail from Montana resident Diane.

Our family has been sighting one or two of what we have started calling Thunderbirds, since we see them just before the thunderstorms. ... We live on a farm in North Central Montana along the Missouri River. There are almost cliff-like hills along the river, [near] which the eagles also enjoy ... catching updrafts. These birds are huge, [with] perhaps fifteen-foot wingspans. They are dark brown, gray—all one solid color. The bottom jaw has a downward curve that is quite noticeable. The wings are long and relatively slim and show a noticeable joint where the wings would fold. I am not sure whether there

were feathers or not, but [what the wings had was] not
unlike the noticeable fingerlike feathers in eagles' wings.
Their legs are not long, nor do they have long tails. The
creepy thing about them is that they give the impression
of being prehistoric, and everyone in our family that has
seen them comment on the evil feeling one gets from seeing them, like the hair on the back of one's neck standing up! We have been noticing them the past two to three
years. They seem to be nesting in some rough land along
the river. So far we haven't found any pictures on the Internet that seem just like what we are seeing.

Wyoming's Winged Wonders

Following my 2009 appearance on the nationally syndicated
radio program *Coast to Coast AM,* I heard an amazing story
from a man named Robert Ward.

About fifteen years ago on a back road in Wyoming, I
was three feet from a Thunderbird. It was a golden eagle
with a height of about five feet and a wingspan as long
as my Astro van. I was driving to a site to repair some
medical equipment. There was a light snowstorm going,
and I was on the radio with a trucker driving behind me.
Up ahead of me it looked like a child was in the middle
of nowhere in this storm. As we slowed to see what was
going on, there were two golden eagles about two-and-
a-half feet tall eating road kill, and this Thunderbird was
easily two times the size of the other birds. I stopped and
it looked at me eye to eye, straight across. Then it opened
its wings and slowly fell away with the two other birds

following it. The truck driver and I were stunned at the size of the animal. Its beak was the size of a large human hand and the claws were a little bigger than that. The bird could easily carry away a small child or a small deer.

My follow-up interview with Ward revealed that his sighting took place on Highway 30, between the communities of Kemmerer and Granger. Remarkably, in 2013 I received a corroborating e-mail from a woman named Kelly, who lives a mere forty miles south of where Ward had seen the father of all eagles.

I just wanted to let you know that in August of 1976 my mother and I saw the big bird in Mountain View, Wyoming, at our ranch. We have never told this to anyone. But I sure am glad that someone else had sighted it …

Colorado's Colossal Birds

I include here an e-mail that contains some frankly fantastic allegations from a Colorado resident by the name of Charles.

Eight years ago I saw a jet-black Thunderbird … next to the escarpment of South Table Mountain near Golden, Colorado. I was about three-quarters of a mile away, driving on the highway when an absolute 747 of birds flew by. It was riding a thermal from a thunderstorm. The Thunderbird's wingspan was thirty-six feet. I think it was a huge turkey vulture … and holy cow, it was huge. … Its talons looked like horse legs hanging down. … This bird was big enough to pick up a baby deer, if not an adult. It changed the alignment of its wings as a glider and rolled over South Table Mountain. It was a really incredible thing to see … I think there are also remnants of a Thunderbird mural on the mountain.

Another Colorado report appeared on the ever-popular (but currently defunct) *Cryptozoology.com* website in 2007. It had been submitted by a woman named Jenelle.

On July 4th, my boyfriend and I were driving from Valmont & 30th Street West, toward Broadway so we could watch the fireworks. We ended up taking Balsam up to NW Boulder, and I was leisurely appreciating the weather, and hoping it was going to rain (no I am not joking, they were saying it was going to thunder after the fireworks). Just a little background, we go hiking regularly at different elevations, and so I can say we both have a good sense of dimension. In addition, we are VERY avid bird lovers (nerds, nerds, nerds)! I look up, and there is this HUGE raptor bird, dark brown, with bronze sheen on the wing coverts. Only once did it fly down closer to the trees. My gosh, I cannot even accurately state the wingspan, but I have seen plenty of hawks, vultures, parrots, condors, and it was much larger.

The author sits next to a life-size
teratorn statue at the San Diego Zoo.

Golden State Thunderbird

In California's La Brea Tar Pits, there have been hundreds of fossilized bones found that evidently remain from the wondrous prehistoric teratorn birds. Interestingly, a man named Bill Clary from Rancho Cordova, California, contacted me in order to inform me about a huge bird he sighted way back in 1967. At the time, he was a sophomore in high school and was approximately fifteen years old. Clary was learning how to drive that particular summer and was traveling with his instructor on Highway 49 somewhere between Placerville and Auburn. As he looked to his left up a steep hill, he caught a glimpse of a huge bird perched on a thick tree limb about seventy to eighty yards away. His impression was that the animal was dark brown in color and possessed the general shape of an eagle, though it looked to be around six feet tall, which is about twice the height of a typical eagle. This made him do a double take. The bird seemed to be looking around and surveying its surroundings. Clary recalled that it was a clear morning at the time, with excellent visibility. Due to the fact that he was in training and in the charge of his driving teacher, he was unable to stop and get a better look. When I interviewed him over the phone, I felt as though the event had a profound impact on him at the time and that, as a result, his recollection was still quite vivid even forty-some years later.

The Big Bird Returns

Beginning in 2008, I investigated a few seemingly corroborative big bird reports stemming from a reasonably concentrated area that extends from far northeast in Texas into adjacent, western Arkansas. As an investigator, one is always hoping to discern patterns that will build a stronger case. It is my opinion that the proximity and timing of these accounts is compelling, particularly since they come from unrelated sources.

The first sighting to be brought to my attention took place in Upshur County, Texas, and involved a woman named Carrie Dugan. According to Dugan's testimony, on the afternoon of January 12, 2008, a massive black bird flew over her property, literally dwarfing the large vultures and eagles she had observed there on numerous occasions. Dugan was so excited that she actually called her husband at work in order to tell him about what had happened. And although he initially felt like she may have been telling him a "big fish tale," after a while he apparently became convinced by her sincerity. Dugan told me that even from a distance of 300 yards, she could tell that the bird's wingspan overreached several old-growth pine trees, indicating that the thing was enormous.

Just over two years later during the summer of 2010, I received a notification from a woman named Liz whose husband and son had witnessed a huge bird flying over and then landing in their pasture just outside of Sims, Arkansas, in the Ouachita National Forest. This is less than 200 miles northeast of where Dugan had her sighting, not a considerable distance for an enormous bird to have traveled in that time period. The witnesses described a mostly black bird with a white head, except that the wingspan was estimated to be between fifteen and twenty feet, at least twice as big as a bald eagle.

Within two weeks of the Arkansas encounter, I also heard from a Mesquite resident named Michael Minadeo who had seen a miraculous bird flying over Dallas, Texas, on the evening of August 11, 2010. At first Minadeo had considered the object to be an airplane, but as he watched it soaring overhead he realized that it was in fact a living creature possessing an eagle-shaped head and appearing to be entirely black in color. Minadeo was so anxious to locate other people who had seen the thing that he actually posted an advertisement on the website Craigslist.

Also of particular interest is the 2010 e-mail that I received from a resident of Tyler, Texas, named Edward who informed me that his mother-in-law had seen a five- or six-foot-tall bird of prey standing in her backyard one evening during 2007. Tyler is only about 40 miles southwest of where Carrie Dugan's property is located and is in the same general region as the other accounts. Furthermore, there is a story about an immense and threatening gray bird that was killed just to the north in Coal County, Oklahoma, during the 1850s. Those who examined the animal's remains recalled that it smelled horrible and had a sixteen-foot wingspan.

This is merely a sample size of potentially related incidents. However, I am firmly convinced that the vast majority of people who have encountered these monster birds are reticent to talk about their experiences, either because they do not realize that they have seen something wholly undocumented, or perhaps like Carrie Dugan, they are fearful of being considered either a bit delusional or dishonest. If this is the case, we must wonder how many Thunderbird encounters go unreported.

Condors in a Cornfield?

Stop the presses! As I was putting the final touches on the manuscript for this book, I was just informed of a potential Thunderbird sighting from, of all places, northwestern Iowa, proving that this is an ongoing phenomenon that seems to know no geographic boundaries. On an early November afternoon between 1981 and 1984, a man named Darry Hartsock was pheasant hunting with his father outside their farmhouse when they noticed two improbable birds standing tall in the middle of a field about a third of a mile away. This particular incident occurred near Pilot Creek and the towns of Havelock and Mallard. Because the figures were adjacent to corn stalks, Darry was able to estimate that the raptors easily stood four to five feet tall. Despite the great distance, the experienced outdoorsmen felt sure that the all-black animals were nothing they had ever seen before—definitely not wild turkeys, buzzards, or bald eagles. The birds presented a noticeably slim profile. Hoping to get a better look, Darry and his dad decided to dash into the house in order to retrieve some binoculars. But when they returned a few minutes later, the creatures were nowhere to be seen. Darry tells me in retrospect that the only thing that he could equate the things to were giant condors, despite the fact that the closest population of these endangered birds lives over twelve hundred miles away in a diametrically different type of terrain.

Immense Birds in Illinois

For reasons that are not all that apparent, Illinois has a rich tradition of Thunderbird accounts that dates back centuries. Long before the area was settled, unknown people painted two large pictographs on a stone bluff overlooking the Mississippi River near what is now the city of Alton. The colorful murals seemed to depict Chimera-like monsters of a menacing nature and inspired fabulous ideas about what they were actually meant to represent. Writing about them in 1836, professor John Russell of Alton's Shurtleff College referred to the creatures as the *Piasa*, suggesting that the name was derived from a Native dialect and that it translated to "the Bird That Devours Man." In retrospect, Russell may have been concocting a fictional tale, since the word "Piasa" cannot be found in the Illini tribe's vocabulary. Yet, after quarrying in the 1860s caused the famous cliff wall to collapse into the Mississippi, local artists paid tribute by painting a new version of the Piasa just upriver. Russell's article must have resonated with them, since the artists were sure to add on wings, which the original pictographs lacked.

A modern pictograph of the Piasa Bird at Alton, Illinois.

Nevertheless, Illinois boasts at least twenty-three Thunderbird reports since 1948. Without a doubt, the most famous incident occurred in the central town of Lawndale on July 25, 1977, when a young boy named Marlon Lowe was temporarily plucked from the ground by one of two enormous birds flying just overhead. This notable event was verified by a handful of witnesses, including Lowe's parents. Five days later and eighty miles to the south, controversial footage of what appears to be two outsized birds was shot at Lake Shelbyville.

Further verification that something exceptional was flying over the Prairie State during the 1970s came via resident Walter Bednarik, who reached out to me in order to relate the following account.

In the summer of 1976, I was walking on a trail along the banks of Salt Creek in Brookfield (a suburb of Chicago), Illinois, in the forest preserve, when I heard some noise behind me. I was maybe ten feet from the edge of the water. As I turned toward the creek, I saw a large black bird, flying slowly, gliding down the length of the creek. It flew by level with my head, about eight feet above the water.

The bird was dark, all black, with a large wingspan of fifteen to twenty feet, which is the width of the creek in that area, bank to bank. The head was large, same color as the body; its neck was also black, not long like a condor or vulture, but more like an eagle. The wings appeared to be fully extended, and the wing tips had clearly visible individual feathers, just like an eagle. And just as quickly, it flew around the bend in the creek and was gone.

Later that day, I ran into one of the senior bird keepers at Brookfield Zoo that I knew and related my experience. He listened, and his first response was I saw a golden eagle. I reminded him of the wingspan, overall size, and color; then he said maybe a condor. He showed

me one of the eagles in captivity and a picture of a condor, but neither matched the color, wingspan, or size of
what I saw.

There seems to have been a bit of a lull in sightings over the
next dozen years or so, with things getting interesting again in
1990. At least according to eyewitness Jeff Beyers, who claims
to have had a sighting in late November a mere three miles
south of his hometown of Pana. Driving swiftly down Route
51 on a clear, starry night, Beyers spotted what he at first
took to be a man wearing a trench coat standing in the road.
Imagine his surprise when the figure unfurled wings around
fifteen feet across, flapped them once and then disappeared
into the darkness. In that instant, he realized that the subject's
head was clearly that of a great, gray, feathered bird. During
an interview, Beyers admitted that the thing had been "scary
big." Of particular interest in this case is the fact that the location is immediately adjacent to Lake Shelbyville, where the
two mystery birds were filmed in 1977, as well as sixteen miles
due north of the town of Hettrick, where another sighting has
been documented.

At the turn of the century, Illinois resident Kyle Danhausen
had a dramatic encounter.

My friend and I were out hunting...I'd say in 1999,
maybe 2000, near Cabery, Illinois. It was a really cold,
nasty day, and there was a system going through with
real tall clouds. It was blowing and gusting and snow-
ing a little. I would say this was in late November, early
December.... I was just standing there about forty yards

away from my friend just watching the dogs work when I heard him yell, "Look!" There, above us and circling down was a massive bird (which we later decided was trying to kill one of our dogs).... I noticed that the wings...were enormous.... We both agreed it could have been up to a twenty-foot wingspan...I do think the bird had feathers, but I really couldn't tell. It was dark and without color and was fairly long as well. When [my friend] yelled, it saw us and swooped back up into that system that was rolling through the area and was literally gone in seconds. We walked over to each other and both immediately asked if the other had noticed how gigantic the bird was. It was, for years, just a story we told and all of our friends laughed at us... My friend and I have both spent our whole lives in the outdoors, and we didn't know what it was.

So begins a trend of sighting towards the far northern section of the state. An Illinoisan named Ken Fitch alleges to have had an unusual sighting in 2005.

My wife and I were at Rock Cut State Park in northern Illinois when we saw a bird that did not look familiar to us. Having grown up on a farm, I was used to seeing hawks, crows, vultures, eagles, and owls. The bird we saw most resembled a crow but did not fly like one.... What struck us most was the large size of the bird. It had to be three or four times bigger than any hawk or eagle we have seen.... It flew back and forth three times before it went out of sight. Of course we did not have a camera.

The most recent Thunderbird account that I am aware of from any locale occurred on August 14, 2013. That very same day I was contacted by Pamela Hutchings of Naperville in Will County, who wrote,

> My kids and I saw a very large bird fly by our house today, and upon trying to Google what it was I could not find anything... [nor] any answers. My question—Is there really no type of bird here this big, so I can give it a name? It had about a twenty-foot wingspan. It was pure black except tips of the feathers on the wings were lighter (I want to say yellow). I can only say the head looked prehistoric (I know how this sounds). I don't know how to explain it... I wasn't holding my phone to snap a picture. It was not a heron or crane.

Pamela's description of the mystery bird's prehistoric-looking head is worth noting. Many witnesses, including the photographer responsible for the 1977 Lake Shelbyville footage, have made similar remarks about the ancient appearance of these birds, though we must wonder if it is merely a visceral reaction based on the sheer size of the things. In my mind, consistent estimates of fifteen- to twenty-foot wingspans as well as bodies covered in dark feathers seem to rule out cases of misidentification involving known species like common turkey vultures or eagles. Some observers in Illinois have compared what they saw to condors, though the relatively flat terrain of the region would have little appeal for these massive, mountain-dwelling birds. Still, Illinois must be recognized as a state that consistently produces its fair share of encounters.

Michigan's Mystery Birds

While it's not typically a state where Thunderbirds are sighted, I have amassed a handful of reports from Michigan as of late. The primary incident occurred on June 17, 2008, near Niles in the southwestern part of the state and involved a man named Kevin, who wrote,

> Earlier tonight I was in my backyard with my family when my mother and I both at the same time looked up to see an enormous bird fly due west over our house. I have seen hundreds if not thousands of turkey vultures, and this was not one. It was approximately fifty to seventy-five feet above the treetops of mature oak trees, and I looked at the tree, which it disappeared behind, and then looked at where the wing tips were in comparison. Straight below that is a twelve-foot cargo trailer that we have, so I estimate that the bird had at least a twelve-foot wingspan but probably larger. To my knowledge there is nothing in this area of that size.

Giant Raptors of Virginia

For reasons I can only speculate, the state of Virginia has been the source of multiple reports accumulating within my database. In the interest of maintaining a sense of order, I also include here an older, secondhand account originating from the extreme southwestern part of neighboring West Virginia, in Mingo County to be exact. A man named Joseph Davis recalled,

My grandfather, who died in 1973, often told the family about an encounter with a Thunderbird when he was a young man, which would have been in the time period of around 1920.... My grandfather had been hunting with a dog and was startled to see an enormous, Thunderbird-type bird swoop down low over where he was standing in a small clearing. The bird circled back around menacingly and then flew off. My grandfather was a coal miner and pretty fearless character who was not known to tell stories that were not true.

Cruising east into Virginia proper, we have a testimonial from an eyewitness named Heather, who states,

My sister and I were small, but it was in Reston, Virginia, around the early to mid-1970s that we saw two giant black birds the size of two small airplanes... Well, I'm forty-five years old now, and I'm going to say I was at least six years old then. My sister who was with me is thirteen months younger than me. I can only say that we were playing next to a creek, and it was in a clearing, and we happened to see them flying overhead, kinda side by side, and as I recall they were black. I think that their feet and beaks were a lighter color, maybe yellowish, but truthfully I can't remember. They were flying maybe twenty-five or thirty feet above the trees, and as I recall some of those trees were pretty tall. All I can say is they were gigantic birds, but I haven't seen anything like it since, and my sister doesn't deny seeing them but doesn't like to talk about it.... I have found one other person who saw one in the early '90s, but she is now deceased.... It seems that there are more people coming out ... but [I] just needed to find someone that would possibly believe my story.

Without question, one of the most terrifying run-ins with a monstrous bird that I am aware of occurred at a tiny place called Comstock Pond. The story was told to me by a man named Scott Oldmixon, who alleges having an unquestionably harrowing ordeal.

In 1993 when I was eighteen, a friend of mine and I had a close encounter here in Virginia. At first it literally sounded like a herd of deer crashing through the woods with all of the branches breaking. We were in a canoe and the bird literally came right at us. Armed with a 16-gauge shotgun, we shot it at about fifteen feet away. Feathers flew, but the bird did not seem to be affected at all. I know this sounds like something out of a movie, but I would swear on my life it happened.

And finally, fifty miles southeast of Oldmixon's encounter comes a lucid and reasonably current sighting by resident Steven.

I've raised and hunted animals all of my life and can't really explain what I saw on November 16, 2011. I was traveling one afternoon (3:00 p.m., clear weather) on State Route 620 between Smithfield and Petersburg. I observed what can best be described as a large feathered animal standing on the ground hunched over. The animal was no more than ten feet off the side of the road, standing on the edge of a cleared field. For size, the best description I have is it was about the size and color of a large chocolate Labrador retriever.... Just as I was about to stop, the animal essentially stood up from a hunched-over position, turned its head, and looked straight at me. When I realized it wasn't a dog, I basically started to accelerate. I wish I'd taken a photo of the animal, but to be honest once I realized it wasn't a dog, I was really thrown off [by] its size and sort of froze.... It was definitely covered with feathers and wasn't frightened by my proximity.

Though the number of documented eyewitness accounts of monster birds is compelling, physical proof remains elusive. As of yet, no one has been able to produce remains, let alone giant feathers, eggs, nests, or even droppings. Until someone presents this sort of definitive evidence, the Thunderbird will continue to be perceived as merely a myth.

Chapter 6
MODERN DRAGONS

Beyond any doubt, the most influential legend permeating multifarious cultures worldwide is that of the fearsome dragon. Tales of monstrous reptiles capable of wreaking havoc and mass destruction date back at least seven millennia in Chinese antiquity, and some three thousand years ago the ancient Sumerians revered a great, saurian beast known as *Kur*. There's also an entire Old Testament chapter (Job 41) that chronicles a quasi dragon called Leviathan, a titanic beast that dwelt in the oceans and was capable of devouring the world. Even in ancient Mesoamerica, certain indigenous tribes worshipped a winged serpent god named Quetzalcoatl. The archetypal medieval dragon is often portrayed as a winged, fire-breathing ophidian that is often the chief antagonist of some great knight or warrior on a mighty quest. To what do we owe these diverse but seemingly parallel myths? Were the beliefs merely spawned by encounters with outsized crocodilians, snakes, and lizards? Or perchance could there be a connection to the enormous, dragon-like reptiles that ruled our planet sixty-five million years ago?

There is a theory that states that the discovery of fossilized dinosaur bones by early people may have instilled a belief in dragons. Bone fragments from various prehistoric animals are still sold in Chinese apothecaries to this day because they are believed to contain certain medicinal benefits. In fact, these are frequently still referred to as "dragon" bones. The beaked skull and stout quadruped body of a dinosaur called *Protoceratops* is thought to have spawned the legend of the dragon-like griffin. Conceivably, is there any chance that some dinosaur species could have survived the mass Cretaceous extinction event, astounding humans at some point during our distant past? Could a real dragon persist in some remote, mountain lair even to this day?

As mentioned in chapter 4, the 1938 discovery of the coelacanth, an ancient fish that was believed to have gone extinct along with the dinosaurs, stands as a weighty example that extinction is not always a permanent classification once it has been declared. Remember, too, that not all sizable reptiles went extinct at the close of the Mesozoic Era. Crocodilians, some of which can obtain lengths of twenty feet, have survived and have flourished, virtually unchanged since that time. The largest known snakes, pythons, and anacondas are capable of reaching lengths of over twenty feet, and during the Paleocene epoch some snakes (*Titanoboa*) grew twice that long. Goliath species of sea turtles and land tortoises can weigh between 800 and 1,500 pounds. The largest known lizard, the Komodo dragon (*Varanus komodoensis*), can reach lengths of up to ten feet and was hidden from western scientists until only a century ago. Perhaps the notion of a modern dragon is not so far-fetched after all.

*Could giant crocodiles have been responsible
for some dragon myths?*

The Tatzelwurm of the Alps

When I was fifteen years old, my father and I took a bus tour across Switzerland. This memorable adventure unfolded during the idyllic summer of 1982, and one of my truly favorite memories from that time is of attempting some light trekking through the gorgeous Alps mountains. I'll never forget the intoxication I felt upon hearing about an enigmatic local creature referred to as the *Tatzelwurm*. Based on eyewitness descriptions, this elongate, fair-sized animal did not seem to resemble any type of worm at all, since (according to general accounts) it possessed a thick, scaly body; sharp teeth; and at least two limbs. Most curious was the animal's apparent aggression towards innocent passersby, as well as a proclivity to pounce great distances when defending its territory. Some have claimed that the Tatzelwurm emits a hissing sound when threatened, and others that its bite is laced with venom. Oftentimes it is viewed slinking into caves and crevices at higher altitudes. On the surface it certainly sounds as though a sort of dragon survived into present-day Europe.

The author, as a young boy, searches the Swiss Alps
for the Tatzelwurm.

Confrontations with the Tatzelwurm were evidently so commonplace during the early nineteenth century that its image was portrayed in Bavarian field guides of the time. An Austrian hiker logged one of the more memorable sightings as recently as 1933, but run-ins with the Tatzelwurm seem to have diminished dramatically since then. Various suggestions have been put forward for the critter's true identity, since it does not resemble anything that is currently known in that region. One thought is that the Tatzelwurm represents a very large and aggressive burrowing lizard similar to the Gila monster of the American Southwest or perhaps a type of gigantic skink. Another theory holds that it may in fact be a large amphibian, not unlike the giant salamanders of Japan and China. From my perspective, it's not difficult to envision a rare and robust form of European legless or glass lizard (*Pseudopus apodus*) accounting for the Tatzelwurm stories, with the whimsical features (pouncing, venomous) sprinkled in for flavor.

Europe boasts a rich history of dragon tales. For centuries, according to aged literature, the entire continent was virtually crawling with them. Surprisingly though, a smattering of contemporary accounts have surfaced. For example, villagers in Syracuse, Sicily, hunted and eventually shot a huge serpent during December of 1933, according to newspaper articles from the time. The monster had been accused of terrifying the locals, since estimates put the specimen's length at anywhere from eleven to twenty feet. Unfortunately, its remains were burned by its overzealous conquerors. The following year in the forests of Monterosso al Mare, Italy, an elderly man encountered a scaly, green and gold dragon eight feet in length. Some three and a half decades later, an Italian man claimed he was chased by a fifteen-foot, scaly, thick-legged lizard that reminded him of a dinosaur. The witness remarked that the beast seemed to exhale heated breath, a dragon-like attribute to be sure. This occurred near the city of Forlì, Italy, during December of 1970.

In June of 1975, a tomato farmer named Maurizio Tombini was working near Goro, Italy, and was frightened by a reptile that he estimated was ten feet eight inches long and as thick as a good-sized dog. Tombini also noted that the animal possessed four legs and apparently left some impressive tracks on the ground, which were examined by police. Tombini was adamant that what he saw was not a crocodile and the man apparently had a reputation for having a serious disposition. Other residents also encountered the Goro Monster, and a few villagers even claimed that it made a howling sound reminiscent of a wolf.

Neighboring France can declare a modern dragon too. During May of 1939, French women who were picking berries near Ossun encountered a gigantic "lizard." The creature had previously been seen decades earlier, around the 1890s.

Dragons in the New World

One of my very favorite "worlds-colliding" stories involves a South Dakota farmer who claimed that his tractor was run off the road by a "dragon" back in 1934. For weeks prior, the distressed landowner noticed that some of his prized livestock was disappearing without a trace. Then one day he was operating his trusty machinery when something built like a dinosaur supposedly charged right past him. The man watched in disbelief as the creature vanished into nearby Campbell Lake. It left behind a few deep impressions in the muddy shoreline, but there were no other signs of the perplexing intruder. Nor has the beast been seen since, as far as we know.

An equally lively episode involves a Kentucky cryptid known as the Milton Lizard or Canip Monster Lizard. During July of 1975 a peculiar series of events unfolded in the tiny city of Milton, located in Trimble County. On July 3, the local newspaper published a photo of an unidentified animal track located in a tomato field belonging to resident Carl Abbot. The clawed, four-toed print measured four and a half by five inches, and whatever had left it in the soil had allegedly made some aggressive sounds that resonated throughout the evening. There was also the disconcerting matter of a neighborhood dog that had been assaulted by an unseen creature. The pooch had apparently sustained some deep gashes in its side.

Meanwhile, on the northeast side of Milton adjacent to the Ohio River lies meandering Canip Creek as well as (at that time) the Blue Grass Body Shop and auto scrapyard, owned and operated by the Cable brothers, Clarence and Garrett. Clarence, also known as "Toughy," was the first one to spot the animal on their property as it emerged from some debris next to the wreckage of an old van. The alarmed business owner was astonished to observe an immense, man-sized reptile and was duly impressed by its huge, bulging eyes and foot-long forked tongue. The creature appeared to display an off-white color on its underside but had prominent black and white stripes as well as quarter-sized orange specks across its head and back. Its legs were each about eight to ten inches long. Garrett encountered the incomprehensible creature around three weeks later on July 25, after he had detected it slithering through a stockpile of car hoods.

By the time Garrett had returned to the location with his brother, as well as a rifle, the lizard was nowhere to be found. The following day, Toughy encountered the thing again but upped his size estimate to a whopping fifteen feet in length. Feeling threatened, he hurled a rock in its direction, causing the reptile to hiss at him before escaping into the thicket bordering the creek. Toughy returned a few minutes later with his rifle once again and fired into the brush where he had seen the abomination enter, apparently with no result. The brothers were supposedly unsuccessful in finding any volunteers brave enough to help them track the animal down. Ultimately, the

speculation was that the specimen had probably been an escaped varanid (monitor lizard), though it must be recognized
that even the great Komodo dragons of that family rarely grow
longer than ten feet. An on-site inquiry by investigator Mark
A. Hall during 1979 confirmed that the Milton Lizard had utterly vanished.

Some odd yarns originating in the American Southwest
suggest living, two-legged, theropod dinosaurs may be running
about. Virtually all of the accounts are dubious at best. Referred
to as "river dinos" or "mountain boomers," these creatures are
mostly reported from riverbeds and watering holes in either
southern Colorado or southwestern Texas, respectively. The
prototypical version stands anywhere from three to five feet tall
and has green- or gray-colored skin; a relatively small, snakelike head attached to a long neck; vestigial arms; powerful hind
legs; and a stout tail. The things have been compared to large,
upright lizards that are swift and graceful in their movements.
Secondhand tales of these creatures scavenging roadkill or even
running cars off the road sometime during the 1970s prevail.

The original source of the outlandish stories may be traced
back to a letter penned by a woman named Myrtle Snow. Her
testimonial was published in a Sunday supplement called *Empire
Magazine* in 1982. Snow claimed to have seen man-sized dinosaurs no less than four times over the course of her life and at
various points in Colorado and New Mexico. My colleague Nick
Sucik spent considerable time researching the subject in 2005 and
surprisingly uncovered other accounts. During 2001, a woman
and her daughter who were motoring through the Yellow Jacket
area spotted a five-foot river dino near an irrigation canal. They

both felt that the thing looked like a cross between a reptile and bird, though it was completely featherless. The animal had a serpentine neck, thin legs and two stubby arms extending forward just below its neck area. Sucik also investigated an earlier account from 1996 that involved a woman living in Kampark near Mesa Verde. The witness happened to glance outside and noticed a reptile that she couldn't identify running swiftly by. Sporting a cone-shaped snout and prominent tail, the creature stood three and a half feet tall and was clearly on two legs.

Texas *T. rex*?

Having once addressed Texas's dinosaurian mountain boomers in a rather incredulous fashion, I resolved to file the whole matter away in my folder with other improbable scenarios and B-sides. Imagine my surprise when I was contacted by Lon Strickler, a resourceful researcher who runs a popular website called *Phantoms and Monsters*. Strickler felt that I might harbor a genuine interest in certain recent events that had transpired in far southern Texas and revolved around reports of small dinosaurs. Boy, was he right! The area in question was familiar to me, as I had scoured the Rio Grande Valley a decade ago while investigating abundant accounts of pterodactyl-like creatures. The valley is a very different kind of place in terms of its culture and habitat.

The sightings came about during the summer of 2013, and the descriptions seemed astoundingly similar to those of the boomers that I had so casually dismissed in my book *Monsters of Texas* (coauthored with Nick Redfern). Hebbronville resident Michelle Raines recalled,

My friend actually saw a small dinosaur here in town on a main street! It was evening when she saw it, probably around 8:45 p.m. She was driving and noticed the dinosaur crossing the street! She saw the shape clearly as it passed another car's headlights on the opposite side. She said oddly that the other car didn't seem to notice as the creature passed. She tried to call me but her phone was out of minutes.

It appears as though the encounter may have served as a kind of validation for Raines, who had desperately been trying to make sense of her own troubling episode.

Just a couple of months before I had actually heard the creature I could only describe as a dinosaur. I had been asleep, it was night, maybe around 1 or 2 am. I had awoken and just at that moment I heard an unfamiliar screech of something running by my window. We have an AC unit in the window so the window is basically open. I heard its footsteps as it ran by and it was heavy, whatever it was. I could hear it clearly on the ground. As it ran further away I could hear it screech again! It was like nothing I've ever heard in my life! It was loud too and I wonder if anyone else heard it or saw it. I live in an apartment complex. I just laid there in bed completely bewildered by what I had just heard. I questioned my sanity and if I had heard what I thought I heard. So when my friend saw the "dinosaur," she was excited and wanted to tell me because of what I heard. I'm only sad I didn't get to see it too.

Strickler's subsequent release of Raines's claims on his website and radio broadcast elicited a surprising response: yet another South Texas resident, with the initials L. M., came forward, presumably relieved to have some corroboration.

This morning I was, told by my neighbor that you [Strickler] had received reports of small T-Rex dinosaurs seen in Hebbronville, TX, and you mentioned it on a radio show. I live near Falfurrias, TX which is about 18 miles east of Hebbronville. I and others have seen those creatures. My neighbor and I saw a pair in December 2012 on the roadway behind our houses. We were scared to report our sighting. I know other people in this area have seen the same creatures.

A family member from Sabinas Hidalgo in Mexico told me that he saw a "big lizard" the last time he visited us. He saw it while he was driving near McAllen, TX. He described the same thing we have seen. It was 2–3 ft. tall with a large head and long tail. It ran on 2 legs and was very dark in color. The two creatures we saw were dark brown and walking quickly on 2 legs also. It was about 4:30 pm and we watched them for about 20 seconds as the moved towards the dead end of the road. We got a very good look.

For a few nights after that, we heard short shrills coming from the brush at the end of the road.

A couple of weeks later, my son told me that he and his friends found many quail feathers and deer bones scattered by a tree in the same brush. I did contact a wildlife authority about the remains but didn't mention what we had seen. He said it was probably coyotes, though I have not heard or seen coyotes for a long time. Another neighbor lost a dog about the same time. Again coyotes were said to be the predator. No remains were ever found. My husband was alarmed and had a high heavy duty steel link fence built around the yard so that our grand children and pets are safe.

… Our dog (Rottweiler) has been acting strange lately. He acts calm and fearless sometimes, but hides and whines other times. This always happens at night. I think these creatures are around again.

Is there a gang of renegade dinosaurs running loose across the southern Texas scrub, or is it perhaps an unknown type of large, bipedal lizard? I plan on pursuing the matter in the very near future.

Twentieth-Century Pterosaurs

When deliberating the archetype of the classical, winged dragon, it is difficult to ignore the physical similarities to the dragon-like, flying reptiles that dominated our planet's skies for 135 million years or so. I am referring of course to the tantalizing pterosaurs, those highly specialized contemporaries of the dinosaurs, some of which (the pterodactyls) obtained airplane-sized dimensions. These creatures possessed membranous bat-like wings, a beak brimming with sharp little teeth, and in some cases ornate head crests or serpentine tails. One can only imagine the types of mythologies these esoteric animals might have spawned if they had outlived their presumed extinction date of sixty-five million years ago. There are a surprising number of people who have claimed to have seen these prehistoric animals alive and well in modern times.

Acting on a tip, I contacted an Arizona woman named Elvia who believes she encountered an enigmatic, winged entity years ago. According to Elvia's testimony, the event occurred between Victorville and Phelan, California, sometime back in 1982 or 1983. At the time she was working at a market that closed around 9:00 p.m., and after shutting it down with a fellow employee one evening, Elvia began her drive home on a remote road through the desert. During our interview, she recalled that it was pitch black outside and described the road as basically a wide, gravel trail running alongside a ditch. She was steering her half-ton, bobtail pickup truck, when a humongous beast bigger than her vehicle suddenly passed overhead. According to Elvia, the "bird" didn't appear to have any feathers, though it possessed an extremely pointy head. She perceived a gray and pink pattern under its wings, which she estimated to be twenty-five feet across. Immediately following the incident, Elvia considered turning around and going back to the spot in order to get another look at the thing but thought about her children and decided it was not worth the risk.

A corroborating incident involves a young woman named Rhiannon Smith who saw something she interpreted as a pterosaur during 2003 or 2004. Smith's sighting took place just outside of Lancaster, California, only forty miles west of Elvia's encounter. Smith recalled,

I noticed a large winged creature off the left of the freeway. Judging the distance, I would have to say it was probably about 150 feet away…but the creature was definitely large enough for me to get a very good look at it. There were no feathers whatsoever, and the creature had large, leathery-type wings. It did not have a large crest on its head like a pteranodon, but it had the characteristic bald head and long beak like a pterodactyl. I honestly cannot remember if it had a short or long, thin tail, and I wish for the life of me I could remember.…I thought, surely I must be hallucinating or something, but I watched the creature silently glide between two hillsides and some trees for about a good ten seconds at least. I was so startled and shocked that I yelled to my parents, "Hey, look!" But soon stopped after I realized they wouldn't believe me and would probably think I was imagining it. Sometimes to this very day I wonder if I was just seeing a figment of my imagination, but I'm not one to make up random things and pretend they are real.…I've always been one of those "I'll believe it when I see it" type [of] people. Well, I guess my motto is true. I know what I saw and no one can say it was a bird, or small airplane, or whatever.…A pterodactyl is exactly what it looked like.…I saw it with my own two eyes.…It was just so surreal.

Rounding out our southern California cluster, we have this account from a resident of Oxnard who I'll call James:

In late May of 2008, it was dusk, and I was out with my telescope. During a break from the scope, I looked up to see two flying creatures that appeared slightly anomalous to me. I have some experience estimating altitude from flying small aircraft, and I would estimate that what I saw was approximately 800 feet above sea level, flying south-southwest. They were in a steady glide; [they made] no power strokes or wing beats like a bird would. I was a bit taken aback. I saw two creatures, flying in a right-wingman formation. They didn't look quite like birds: the wings were the wrong shape, they didn't have any clearly visible feathering, there were two legs trailing behind them, and they had a strangely shaped head ... I couldn't immediately figure out what they were. Nothing seemed to fit. I pondered this and researched on the Internet for three days before I finalized my opinion of what I had seen. I'm convinced that I saw two pterosaurs that evening in May. I don't make this statement flippantly. I'm quite certain of what I saw, and have taken every step to make sure I am not being misled by my own eyes. It's quite obvious to me that these creatures are still with us.

Up the Pacific Coast about 700 miles or so, the accounts continue. A heart-stopping one occurred during the 1970s, according to Ashland, Oregon, resident Larry.

I saw a giant, prehistoric bird while hunting deer with my cousin in 1973. I was sixteen. He was eighteen. It was latched onto the side of a tall redwood tree [at] about 9:00 a.m. We were high up in the mountains. They were cutting new logging roads into places no one had ever been. We walked into a small clearing on the back side of a mountain. We had no idea it was there. High up that massive tree ... all hell broke loose when I took a couple of steps toward the tree it was clinging to.... It pushed off from the side of the tree to gain flight with such force, such unbelievable power. I heard a crack like thunder break, then silence and a massive *swoosh*. I looked up and the redwood was swaying back and forth ... and it was split right down the middle. I looked to the left and saw it for the first time.... It was not a bird, as we know them to be. It looked truly prehistoric! It made no sound at all, other than the sound of its wings ... [and] it looked to be thirty-five to forty-plus feet from wing tip to wing tip and thirty-plus feet long from beak to tail and about eight-plus feet wide at the midsection.... It had no feathers at all! It looked like it had the skin of an alligator or elephant, darkish gray, and it looked to have twelve-inch square sections all over it like scales, or armor plates, as it were. It did not flap its wings like a bird does but lifted them up high and then down with massive power, and it would shoot forward with each stroke.... I raised my rifle and fired two or three times at it as it took its leave.... [I'm] not sure if I hit it or not. Three or four flaps of its wings and it was gone down the canyon.

Finishing up our West Coast tour, here's a fairly recent 2010 sighting by Troutdale, Oregon, resident Shawn:

I listened to you on *Coast to Coast AM* the other night, and you had asked anyone who has seen a pterodactyl to contact you. I have not only seen one but was within twenty feet of it. I am an avid bird-watcher and I work out of my house, so I am able to take frequent breaks on my deck. I spotted what appeared to be a heron flying from the south, in the early morning, midweek in the spring.... What was perplexing is that I could see the bird, but it was still a great distance off. I knew it was large, but my only reference up to this point was a heron, so it did not make any sense that the bird had not arrived at my location given a normal time frame.... When I went back out, I could see the enormous size of this thing, and then it had my attention. The best I can describe the size is about the length of a VW Bug with a large wingspan.... The closer it got the more aware of the size I became.... Now this thing is flying at treetop level, which at the time would be fifteen to twenty feet above me, standing on a second story deck, so I am watching but having trouble processing what is going on. Now I am looking directly at the creature, and it rolls its head sideways to look at me, and the eye moved in the socket and then there we were eyeball to eyeball.... I can remember thinking, *Man, the pterodactyl drawings that I had seen were spot on— the head, the teeth, and the wings with protruding fingers.*

Desert Dragons

Within the annals of Forteana, there is a controversial affair said to have taken place in southern Arizona's arid desert during the late nineteenth century. According to an article that was published in the *Tombstone Epitaph* on April 26, 1886, local ranchers shot a leather-winged monstrosity with a crocodilian head. There's even a widespread belief that the men spread the animal out against the side of a barn and took a photo with it. The problem is though some claimed to have gazed upon this iconic image, no one seems to be able to produce a copy of it or can even recall where the darn thing was published to begin with. The Internet is littered with hoaxed recreations of the scene. Regardless, there seems to be an attitude that winged reptiles might still be found in the vast barren deserts of the American Southwest. Towards the end of 2011, I received correspondence from a young woman named Pamela Marsh indicating that may be the case.

> We were driving from a new house my parents bought in Alto and noticed this tan-looking bird that resembled a pterodactyl flying in a field.... We didn't get to see where it actually went. It wasn't very big like some people have reported (looking like small airplanes), but [it was] a smaller version. I saw it along with my son and mom. This is the weirdest thing I have ever seen in my life. We saw ... this pointed-head bird flying.... It just seemed like its head, beak, and [the] point on [its] head [were] more narrow. It went pretty fast, and we only noticed its wings and head and can't recall looking

at the tail.... We will always remember that this is not a normal bird.

Pterodactyls over Texas

In my first book, *Big Bird!: Modern Sightings of Flying Monsters*, I examined the lengthy history of winged creature sightings throughout my home state of Texas. In particular, the American Bicentennial year of 1976 seemed to produce a dramatic number of reports, though descriptions of the animals in question vacillated between monstrous black raptors and bat-winged pterosaurs. Occasionally, I still receive provocative testimonials such as this one sent to me by Texas resident Fiona:

> Both my ex-husband and I saw a giant bird over Houston, Texas, in '76. It was quite close and looked like a pterodactyl. I'll never forget the huge size of it, the enormous wingspan, the clearly defined point at the back of the skull, and the long legs trailing behind. It wasn't just gliding it was smoothly flapping its wings. I saw it as I was looking out the patio door and called my husband to come take a look. He saw it too and tried to call a radio or TV station, but they wouldn't believe him. I didn't know anyone else had seen any giant birds like this until I saw the documentary a couple of years ago on TV, which told of all the giant bird sightings in Texas in the mid-1970s. It was gratifying to find out that others had seen the giants as well. The skeptics try to say it was a giant condor or something like that. It wasn't. You could clearly see the long, slim neck, pointed beak, pointed skull, and long, slim legs. I think of it

as my UFO, as I now know what it feels like to try and tell others of something that sounds impossible and they don't believe you.

My hometown of San Antonio seems to produce a notable number of pterosaur sightings for some reason, perhaps due to its proximity to remote, mountainous areas of Northern Mexico. Over the years, I've amassed reports from a diverse sample of its residents, including law enforcement officers, teachers, a biology student, and even celebrities. Quite recently, I spoke to an ex-Navy sailor named Ismael Wylie, who claims that he saw one of the creatures fly over his property on Christmas Day 2013.

According to Ismael, it was just before 1:00 p.m. He was in his backyard on the far north side of town finishing some yard work when he looked up and spotted what he thought was some type of stork flying his way. Ismael was about to go inside but decided to wait a few moments and enjoy the rare wildlife encounter. As the creature passed about thirty feet directly over his head, Ismael looked up, and only then did he surmise that the animal was not a bird at all but what he perceived to be a living, breathing pterosaur. The thing displayed a relatively small head that was attached to a long, rigid neck. But, what really caught Wylie's attention was its membranous wings, which seemed devoid of feathers with sharp angles and also displayed a pronounced skeletal structure. In addition, the beast exhibited a solid, dark gray or charcoal color that confirmed that it was not a stork, crane, or heron. Ismael's vast experience working in print shops enabled him to later apply an artistic eye and sketch what he had observed.

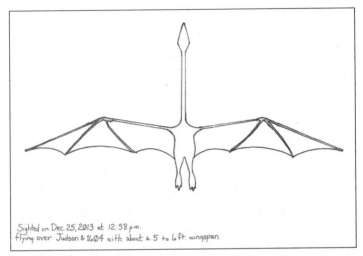

Sighted on Dec. 25, 2013 at 12:58 p.m. flying over Judson & 1604 with about a 5 to 6 ft. wingspan.

Ismael Wylie's sketch of a pterosaur sighted over San Antonio.

Wylie was aware of another incident involving a living pterosaur—and one of reportedly huge stature, to boot. During the early 1990s, while stationed on the USS *Jouett* (CG-29), a 547-foot Naval cruiser, he was awakened by news of an enormous "pterodactyl," which apparently flew overhead in the presence of some fifty to one hundred fellow crewmembers. The location was somewhere in the East Indian Ocean just north of Australia. The significance of this episode is underscored by the fact that the nearby island of Papua New Guinea has long been rumored to be inhabited by a species of winged dragon known as the *ropen*, *duah*, or *indava* bird. Descriptions of this creature jibe well with archaic airborne reptiles, and one could hardly hope for a better habitat to conceal a population of Cretaceous survivors. My friend and colleague Paul Nation of Texas has undertaken no less than four expeditions to New

Guinea in search of evidence and has interviewed many locals who claim to have had encounters. Perhaps the most startling fact about these monsters is the allegation that they are
capable of emitting a bioluminescent glow in the night skies.
Regarding the mass sighting from the USS *Jouett*, it is believed
by some that it was covered up as part of some vast conspiracy.
To any of the ship's crewmembers reading this: I'd love to hear
from you.

Missouri Mystery

I must also mention the American heartland and specifically
the state of Missouri as a place where massive and mysterious
flying things have been encountered. For example, there's the
remarkable experience of a woman named Georgia Brasher
who grew up on a 700-acre farm in the far southeast corner of
the state. Brasher wrote me a letter in order to enlighten me
about a chilling experience she had at age twelve or thirteen
while riding her dirt bike near a big ditch on the edge of the
property:

> As I got closer to the tree line, I saw two huge black ob-
> jects on two of the trees. One was bigger than the other
> one. My mind did not register that these two huge objects
> were birds. I thought something must have come off a
> plane and landed in the trees. The reason I thought that
> was the way the tree was bowed over. It was heavy and
> weighing down the tree.... The closer I got, it looked less
> and less like airplane parts.... All of a sudden the bigger
> one opened up its wings and hovered off the tree. I could
> not believe I was looking at giant birds. My immediate

first thought was [that this was] some prehistoric stuff. They didn't look like they had feathers. It looked like skin when the wings opened, and the span of the wings was enough to scare me ... They never took their eyes off of me. I wasn't close enough to see detail in the face, but they had very long, bony-looking shapes. I felt like I was being sized up, and I knew that the size of those birds could have done me real harm. I got back on my bike and bugged out. I was looking back the whole time expecting to see them swooping down on me, but they stayed on the tree.... When I got back, I was ranting like a crazy person, begging my mom to drive out there and take a look. She would have none of it.... I didn't take my eyes off the skies for a very long time.

Dixie Dragons

As we continue to tour the United States, it appears that there is no region immune to these present-day pterosaur accounts, not even the swampy hills and hollers of the Deep South. While some of these areas remain pretty rugged, I would hardly characterize them as lost worlds. Nonetheless, I'm familiar with an intriguing cluster of sightings originating in parts of northern Georgia and adjacent Tennessee. A woman named Linda mentioned in passing, "I saw a large pterodactyl creature rising out of the woods near Nashville, Tennessee, in 1975.... [Its] wingspan must have been about thirty feet ... [but] unfortunately I had no camera."

During the summer of 2012, a more specific narrative came to light. In this particular instance I was contacted by a woman named Lisa Letanosky who seemed a bit distraught:

I live in Clinton, Tennessee. I just saw a bird that was the most interesting bird I have ever seen. It was huge. It looked like a pterodactyl. You could see the skeleton of its arms and there was no fur or feathers on the underside of its belly, which looked to be the skin of a dragon like you see in a science fiction movie. Small head... [and] there was a large flap of skin hanging down under its chin. It left a huge shadow over the house, as it flew over.... All I could do is say, "What in the [world] is that?" It was around maybe 4:00 or 5:00 p.m. when it was spotted by me and flew over our home very low, might I add. My brother and neighbor were out here and saw the shadow of it flying over, and they were like, "What in the world?" The neighbor's kid saw it as well. This all happened so fast. I ran to the backyard to see it again, but we have a lot of trees back there, and it was already gone. I'm not one to say I saw something if I didn't. I'm as shocked as anyone to know this kind of bird actually exists.

We must acknowledge that some witnesses will mistakenly refer to these animals as birds, a gross generalization based upon superficial design as well as lack of familiarity with the differences. We know from fossils that some pterosaurs looked very similar to birds as a result of convergent evolution, and some even had feather-like structures called pycnofibres on their bodes. As members of the diapsid clade archosauria, pterosaurs and birds are in fact related.

Merely 150 miles due south of Clinton (as the pterodactyl flies), we learn of a potentially related series of events from

Towns County, Georgia. In thoughtful correspondence, a man named David Schroder elaborates,

> I have seen these birds here in North Georgia that are what I believe to be in the pterosaur family. I have seen three in the past three years.... In July of 2010, I saw what appeared to be a mating pair flying north. At their closest point to me they were just one hundred feet above the treetops... directly behind where I work and live. Dark gray skin color like an elephant and featherless, they had what looked to be long, thin tails with a larger area at the end. The heads were long and came to a sharp point, and the only thing that I could compare their look to would be a bat, except for the head and tail. The wingspan—I can only guess from the tree's size—was around fifteen to twenty feet. Anyway, two days ago on December 8, 2012, I and two others were standing outside when a motion in the sky caught my eye. I pointed and said, "What's that?" We all watched what I know was a young pterosaur flying right in front of us. It was just above the treetops in almost exactly the same path that I saw the other two, about a year and a half ago, only it was flying in a southeasterly direction. I know that they are supposed to be nocturnal, but my theory is that the drought here in Georgia has put stress on their environment and has forced them to veer from their normal habits.... The 2010 sighting is not where it started for me; it was about five years earlier. After fighting with myself as to whether what I

know I saw could be real or not, this latest sighting has ended that debate for me.... They are still with us.

During a lengthy phone interview, Schroder impressed me as a man who was terribly sincere in his convictions. His description of long tails with a flattened flange on the end is clearly indicative of certain early pterosaurs (rhamphorhynchoids) and no other known species. Schroder stressed the importance of someone mounting an investigation into the adjacent wilderness in order to look for physical evidence, pointing out that the surrounding areas contain an abundance of water, wildlife, and even cave systems beneficial to concealing a small group of these remarkable creatures. He also mentioned that he believed he had heard an abrupt and aggressive screaming that might be associated with these animals.

Three very recent sightings occurred 125 miles to the southwest of Towns County in the city of Douglasville, Georgia, during 2014. A resident by the name of Christie Parker could hardly contain her excitement in her e-mail to me:

My boyfriend, Maurice, and I were driving down I-20 West [in] Douglasville, Georgia, and we saw a pterosaur in flight. Today was the second time this week. I saw it back in April and it almost crashed into my car, but I didn't know that's what it was since it was 5:30 a.m. and still dark outside. It's incredible! It had no feathers and a long tail with a bulb at the end. The head had a long piece going toward the back. We saw it again an hour or so ago. It must live in this area. We didn't get a chance to take a photo. It was fast.

During a phone interview, Parker and her boyfriend were both adamant that the animal they ultimately sighted on three separate occasions (while driving through roughly the same area) was not a bird. They stressed that the thing was huge, so much so that they could actually see that it had teeth. They both emphasized its unusual "wiggling" tail and head crest as well as the fact that it did not possess feathers.

The relative proximity of these sighting locations in addition to the startling similarity of physical descriptions from unrelated sources is intriguing to say the least. Living pterosaur researcher Jonathan Whitcomb has collected a handful of other corroborating reports from Georgia, South Carolina, and Florida in recent years, indicating that there is strong evidence for Deep South pterosaurs.

Flyers on the Fringe

The nearer we drift to the densely populated metropolitan region stretching from the Atlantic coast to the Midwest United States, the less I expect us to find unfamiliar fauna of any type, especially sizable prehistoric beasts. The only conceivable pitfall in embracing this line of logic is that we are inclined to overlook the fact that the majority of humans inhabit populated areas, leaving tracts of less traveled woodland in between. Some of these territories remain pretty pristine and could present an ideal stopover point for our hypothetical pterosaurs.

Manistee National Forest on the western edge of Michigan may constitute just such a refuge, at least if we consider the testimony of lifelong outdoorsman Hunter Dodge, who claims to have witnessed an unnerving spectacle there during 2009. Dodge was enjoying a fishing excursion at the time. While wading in the middle of a shallow river and casting his line for salmon, the calmness of his morning was shattered by a blood-curdling shriek downriver. The shrill sound repeated rapidly, and then a lower-pitched guttural noise echoed; still he was not able to perceive what was causing it. He did notice that the surrounding forest became eerily silent and lacked the ambient buzz he was accustomed to. A moment later, he caught sight of a winged animal about 300 yards away and some 300 feet above the treetops. Drawing upon his vast experience in the outdoors, Dodge figured that the subject displayed a span between fifteen and twenty feet across and was about twenty to twenty-five feet in length from nose to tail, with the tail being excessively long. Visibility was low, so he struggled to make out the details of the animal's finer points. Despite its bird-shaped wings, Dodge got the distinct impression that the thing was completely featherless and more or less resembled a living pterodactyl. Seconds later, the interloper performed a barrel roll and disappeared into the heavens.

As if this ordeal was not alarming enough, Dodge also con-fided in me that his brother might have actually been attacked by one of the creatures. It was the autumn following his sight-ing, and the two siblings were vacationing at a deer- hunting camp in the Baldwin area a mere thirty-five miles to the north. Just after dark, his brother had wandered into the adjacent woods in order to forage for firewood. All at once there was a thunderous crack followed by deathly silence. Dodge and a friend who was with them at the time rushed into the for-est and discovered his brother sitting in a dazed and slumped over position in the middle of an open field. He had a nasty laceration on his skull as well as a chunk missing from his tongue. The troublesome part is that the brother had (and still has) no earthly memory of what happened to him that night, though his injuries required several stitches and continue to produce residual pain. Dodge points out the proximity of the location to the spot where he sighted his winged abomination and can think of no other reason why his brother would have been harmed in that way other than by an assault from above. Considering that there have been historical accounts of humans being attacked by sinister, winged monsters, it makes one wonder.

Drifting eastward, the state of Pennsylvania boasts a legacy of winged-creature accounts dating back to the late nineteenth century. Traditionally, these mystery beasts have been referred to as Thunderbirds because the accounts typically portray huge, dark-colored buzzards. However, there seems to be some diversity, as evidenced by this 2009 report I received from a resident named Daniel who lives near McConnells Mill State Park in Portersville:

> I don't know where to report something like this, so I figured I'd share this with you. I live in western Pennsylvania and I thought what I saw one night about a year ago was a pterodactyl. When I looked up it seemed to fit the description of what people have called [a] "Thunderbird." Me and my friend were driving down a back road, and it flew over the car and was flying with us about ten feet over the car for about five seconds. It was long enough for each of us to lean forward and look up through the windshield and say, "What the hell is that?" It freaked us out, but I'm positive about what I

saw, and I was talking a few months ago to a friend that lives right around where it happened and swore he saw it one night flying over his yard. He lives in the middle of nowhere. He said it was a twenty-foot-wide wingspan, and that's the size of the one I saw. I know the terrain where these sightings take place, and I know that there's more than enough hiding [space] for a creature like this. It's all caves, hills, and trees. I know they're living there anyway.

In addition to these recent reports, I've chronicled pterosaur accounts from highly populated areas including Maryland and eastern Canada in previous works.

So then, how realistic is it that people are genuinely encountering huge, winged reptiles that vanished from our fossil history tens of millions of years ago? It really comes down to a choice between two equally improbable paradigms: either a substantial number of seemingly credible folks are grossly mistaken, lying, or simply delusional in these matters, or else a breeding population of archaic, flying animals has remained hidden from us (and in the suburbs of one of the most developed nations on earth, at that). If it turns out to be the latter proposition, we will at least have the benefit of knowing that their unlikely survival, no matter how improbable, explains the worldwide dragon legends once and for all.

Chapter 7
MASSIVE AMPHIBIANS

Amphibians have long been one of my favorite groups of animals. Like most lads, I was quite fond of collecting and keeping a diverse assortment of frogs, toads, salamanders, newts, and tadpoles in aquariums and jars while growing up. Looking back, it was probably because I was enamored with their slimy and swampy nature. But as I matured, I began to appreciate what amphibians truly represent to the animal kingdom. You see, they are the honest-to-goodness pioneers of the vertebrates, rejecting their watery origins in search of new opportunities on land. Without this evolutionary gambit, reptiles, birds, and mammals would never have arisen, and I wouldn't be sharing my thoughts on the matter at all. So, bully for the frog!

Most scientists agree that amphibian lineage can be traced back to the Devonian Period, about 370 million years ago. That was long after the first lobe-finned fish had crawled up onto a muddy riverbank and still long before the dinosaurs reigned supreme. Some prehistoric species grew to be quite large and were the apex predators of their time. *Prionosuchus* was a sturdily built specimen that possessed the general form of a crocodile with a robust body that may have weighed as much as 800 pounds, and *Eogyrinus* was an elongate creature that grew to be as long as fifteen feet. However, the largest extant amphibians are the giant salamanders. A Chinese specimen (*Andrias davidianus*) can grow to almost six feet in length, as large as a man. Yet there have been accounts featuring unclassified salamanders and frogs of a truly monstrous nature, and it is these reports that we will ponder in this chapter.

Super Salamanders of the Pacific Northwest

There are three scientifically recognized species of giant salamanders: the aforementioned Chinese type, a closely related species from Japan (*Andrias japonicus*) that is slightly smaller at about four-and-a-half feet in length, and the American hellbender (*Cryptobranchus alleganiensis*), which typically only grows to be about sixteen inches long but can top out at twenty-nine inches. All of these forms appear somewhat similar in that they share broad, flattened bodies with loose, highly folded skin. All three are typically found in the oxygen-rich, swift running water of mountain streams and can thus tolerate colder temperatures. They are essentially ambush predators that primarily feed on small crustaceans, fish, and frogs. However, hellbenders, the only known American species, are strictly native to the eastern states ranging from New York and Pennsylvania down through Alabama and Georgia and have a population ranging as far west as Missouri. Officially, there are no salamanders living in the Pacific Northwest that are larger than a foot in length.

Cryptozoologist Loren Coleman has written extensively about alleged encounters with what could be an unknown population of giant salamanders inhabiting California's Trinity National Forest. The initial incident involved a lawyer named Frank Griffith during the 1920s. Griffith was hunting at the head of the New River when he claimed that he spotted five huge salamanders at the bottom of a pond. Because he recognized that at five to nine feet in length the animals were highly unusual, Griffith apparently attempted to use a large hook in order to pull one of the creatures out but was unsuccessful. Farther south, in 1939 a fisherman netted a large salamander in the Sacramento River and turned it over to Stanford herpetologist George Myers, who identified it as being related to the giant Asian species but with an abnormal brown coloration. There are indications, though, that this particular specimen may have in reality been an escaped pet.

Biologist Thomas Rodgers next looked into the possibility of giant salamanders in the Northwest in 1948, postulating that there could in fact be a relict North American species of giant salamander related to the Asian types. However, Rodgers was unsuccessful in his attempts to locate one. At some point, a colorful animal collector named Vern Harden stated that he had seen a dozen monstrous salamanders at a place called Hubbard Lake and that one had measured over eight feet in length, but Harden's claims were generally disregarded. Still, a number of expeditions ensued from the years 1958 to 1960. Initially, a trip was undertaken by the lake's namesake Father Hubbard himself, and then Texas oil millionaire and adventurer Tom Slick got involved. Finally, three zoology professors from various California colleges made an effort to put an end to the mystery. Decades later in 1997, a search organized by journalist Kyle Mizokami failed to shed any light on the situation. The mystery remains unsolved.

During 2009, a colleague of mine named M. K. Davis, who is widely known for analyzing controversial Bigfoot videos, was on a field trip at Bluff Creek, California, when he supposedly spotted a mottled, three-foot salamander at the bottom of a deep pool. Unaware that such a large amphibian was undocumented on the West Coast (Davis hails from Mississippi), he did not mention the incident until he had left the area. The event later came to light during an interview with blogger Steven Streufert. If Davis was accurate in his estimation of size, his sighting could indicate that California's super salamanders may actually exist.

Based on accounts from up the coast in British Columbia, Canada, the range of these giant amphibians may extend farther north. The first clue surfaced in Ivan Sanderson's book *Abominable Snowmen* when he referenced a letter from a prospector named Charles Flood, who claimed to have seen "alligators" at a small pond in the Holy Cross Mountains along with two other men, Green Hicks and Donald McRae. Flood described the things as being black and about twice the size of lizards. John Kirk of the British Columbia Scientific Cryptozoology Club has gathered multiple reports of something that he suspects are not alligators at all, but rather enormous salamanders ranging from six to a whopping twelve feet in length. Apparently, most of the sightings have taken place at Pitt Lake, though there have been encounters elsewhere, including Chilliwack Lake, Nitnak Lake, and the Fraser River. The most recent and easily most credible account comes from an outdoorsman and guide named Dan Gerak who alleges observing a five-foot, black salamander at the juncture of Pitt Lake and the Fraser River on two different occasions in 2002.

Recently, cryptozoologist Karl P.N. Shuker revealed a promising California sighting from 2005 on his website, *ShukerNature*. An anonymous woman wrote him claiming that she had encountered a four- to five-foot, reddish-brown, mottled salamander with sturdy legs easing down a trail in Redwood Park, Arcata, California, on a damp day. What's more, the witness mentioned that her coworker's boyfriend had seen a similar animal in the area on a different occasion. Given that the Pacific Coast of North America boasts a climate that is comparable to both western China and Japan, an American species of giant urodele (of the order Urodela, which includes salamanders and newts) related to the Asian species is not out of the question. Sadly, this is one of the oft-neglected topics in the field of cryptozoology, though perhaps in time the existence of these huge amphibians will prove to be a reality.

Is Nessie a Newt?

Without a doubt, the most celebrated dragon of the deep is said to inhabit a certain dark and fathomless lake situated in the mist-shrouded highlands of Scotland. I'm referring of course to the Loch Ness Monster, affectionately called Nessie by the locals and the basis of one our very favorite modern mysteries. Accounts are said to date back to 565 CE when none other than Saint Columba faced down the beast. Yet Nessie truly achieved worldwide fame in 1933 when a modern roadway was constructed alongside the lake, granting greater visibility and access. A continuous stream of alleged sightings and photos since that time have painted a romantic portrait of a prehistoric survivor that time forgot. No definitive evidence of the creature's existence has ever been collected, and there are a myriad of theories regarding its true identity—plesiosaur; giant eel; unknown, long-necked seal; primitive, snakelike whale; and huge mollusk are the more common ones. Of course, there are also scores of people who suspect that the entire affair is merely a synthesis of hoaxes and misidentifications of rarely seen natural phenomena.

*Meg Buick's interpretation of the
Loch Ness Monster
as a giant amphibian.*

One idea that perhaps doesn't receive enough consideration is the possibility that Nessie may in fact be some species of colossal amphibian. The late cryptozoologist Roy Mackal, who spent countless hours analyzing the evidence and was an all-around brilliant biologist, hypothesized in 1976 that Nessie might be an immense representative of the order Urodela or perhaps a descendant of the embolomeres, which were sizable, ancient, undulating amphibians that were excellent swimmers. Mackal argued that while most amphibians since the Carboniferous Period have adapted to a largely terrestrial lifestyle, other forms reverted to a primarily aquatic existence. A fifteen-foot specimen similar to the fossil *Eogyrinus* would most definitely qualify as a monster. Amphibians are more comfortable in cold-water environments than reptiles, and because they can breathe by absorbing oxygen through their skin, they would have no great need to come to the surface, where they would be seen. The frigid water of Loch Ness is highly oxygenated, conceivably an ideal environment for this type of denizen.

Following the leads of Mackal and author and explorer William Horsburgh Lane, who first proposed the salamander identity in 1933, other investigators, including Lieutenant Commander Rupert T. Gould, have continued to endorse the virtues of this likelihood. Salamanders are the largest extant amphibians, and proponents of the Nessie-salamander theory often point to an encounter that supposedly happened in 1880. A diver named Duncan McDonald alleged that while searching for a shipwreck in the depths of Loch Ness, he panicked when he almost swam directly into a frightening apparition that (in his opinion) resembled an amphibian of gigantic stature. At the end of the day, Nessie, if it exists, may be nothing more than a titanic newt.

Fredericton's Fabulous Frog

In contrast to salamanders, frogs and toads do not boast a monster-sized representative, at least not that we are aware of. The largest known species is the goliath frog (*Conraua goliath*) of Cameroon and Equatorial Guinea on Africa's Atlantic Coast, which can obtain a length of a foot and a half and a weight of seven pounds. While it's probably something that would make your little sister shriek and shutter in disgust, it certainly is not big enough to swallow her whole. The largest known prehistoric version, the "devil frog" (*Beelzebufo ampinga*) of Madagascar's Cretaceous fauna didn't get much bigger. So then what are the odds that there is a hopping, croaking abomination out there somewhere?

In the collection of a certain museum in Fredericton, New Brunswick, Canada, sits an intriguing exhibit. Known as the Coleman Frog, it is either a fantastic fabrication or else the genuine remains of an amphibian so great that it positively boggles the mind. The unique animal was found at Killarney Lake just north of Fredericton by a man named Fred Coleman in 1885. The frog jumped into Coleman's boat while he was fishing and seemed to warm up to him immediately. He took the creature home with him and, according to the legend, formed a great friendship with the croaking critter, feeding it a combination of June bugs, buttermilk, whey, and whiskey. One rumor states that Coleman gleaned some tips from a French book on how to grow larger frogs. It may have been the unorthodox diet, but the amphibian apparently ballooned in size until it tipped the scale at a whopping forty-two pounds. Ultimately, the famous frog died in a tragic dynamite accident, at which point Fred Coleman sent its remains off to a taxidermist in Bangor, Maine, in order to preserve the marvelous animal for all to admire.

For some time after that, the stuffed specimen supposedly resided at a hotel in Fredericton where disrespectful guests used it as an ashtray. Following a long hiatus, the curiosity was rediscovered in the attic of one of Fred Coleman's heirs and donated to the museum in 1959, where it remains on display to this day. Those who have laid eyes on the thing note its pa-pier-mâché appearance and gaudy green paint job, seemingly revealing it to be nothing more than a clever fake. As remarkable as the entire episode seems, there were evidently credible folks in Fredericton who claim that they saw the huge frog when it was alive; furthermore, we mustn't forget that taxidermy was less advanced in the nineteenth century. In addition, the frog underwent an extensive refurbishment in 1988, resulting in its present patina, which is allegedly distinct from its original color. Common sense indicates that the whole affair is a tall tale, as it's difficult to imagine the laws of nature demonstrating such extreme flexibility. Regardless, it's a moot point since the museum refuses to allow scientists to perform a DNA test. Debate and controversy over the Coleman Frog's authenticity endures.

Loveland Frog

The most celebrated American mystery beast displaying amphibious attributes is Ohio's Loveland Frog—which is perhaps a bit of a misnomer since the accounts include references to upright bipedalism. As a matter of fact, all of the prominent portrayals of this monster adorn it with a distinctly hominid form, not at all a true frog, but more of a "frogman" redolent of Hollywood's *Creature from the Black Lagoon*. Loveland, true to its name, is a warm and pleasant community nestled on the outskirts of Cincinnati. It seems like an idyllic place alongside the scenic Little Miami River, and there exists an indulgent delight in ordaining it the home of a slimy, two-legged goblin that lurks at its fringes late at night. It appears to be a fractured case that combines disparate occurrences that, in the end, muddy our hope for any semblance of a resolution.

The first component is two alleged encounters that seemingly deserve to be classified as UFO literature rather than cryptozoological lore. Prominent UFO researcher and author Leonard Stringfield brought both accounts to notoriety. During August of 1955, one of Stringfield's contacts informed him of a situation that transpired in Loveland a couple of months earlier. A truck driver and civil defense worker named Carlos Flannigan had reported seeing four tiny, humanlike figures behaving suspiciously underneath a bridge that crossed the Little Miami River. He had also detected a stench like alfalfa or almonds permeating the air. When Stringfield, along with UFO investigator Ted Bloecher, traveled to Flannigan's home in order to obtain more information, the witness, who had been largely ridiculed, seemed like he didn't care to revisit the incident:

> [Flannigan] stated that he had only seen four small men with a more or less human appearance, approximately 3 feet tall, and moving in an odd manner under the bridge, seen during no more than 10 seconds. He confirmed that there was then a "terrible odor" at this place. He said nothing else.

But then Loveland Chief of Police John Fritz put the investigators in touch with a local businessman named Robert Hunnicutt who claimed to have had a similar sighting earlier that same year in April. While being interviewed by Stringfield and Bloecher, Hunnicutt explained that he had been motoring through Branch Hill, about three miles southwest of Loveland. It was early around 4:00 a.m. when he observed a trio of three-foot, manlike figures squatting by the side of the road. Thinking there might have been an accident of some kind, Hunnicutt halted his car and waited. Within moments he realized that the beings were not human.

Hunnicutt told his interviewers that these "trolls" were wearing identical gray, tight-fitting jumpsuits and that they also had gray skin. Their long, straight mouths were lipless and frog-like, but they did have human-looking eyes (though lacked eyebrows). Instead of hair they possessed wrinkles on their heads that looked painted on, sort of like on a doll. The entities also sported lopsided chests and long, thin arms, and one of them was clutching a dark object above his head that was shooting out an arc of bluish-white sparks. The last thing Hunnicutt remembered was that the humanoids began moving toward him and waving him away from the scene. A considerable amount of time had passed when he regained his senses while driving to the local police station.

Fast forward to March 3, 1972. While on patrol around 1:00 a.m., Loveland police officer Ray Shockey was cruising along Riverside Drive when he perceived what he thought was an animal, perhaps a dog, lying by the side of the road. As the cop's headlights illuminated the creature, it gawked at him for a few seconds before scaling the guardrail, disappearing behind the obstruction and presumably descending into the bushy thicket that lined the Little Miami River. Despite the brevity of the encounter, Shockey indicated that the specimen was three to four feet in height, weighed at least fifty pounds, had a leather-textured hide, and had a face similar to a frog or lizard with reflective eyes. This was all according to long-time creature investigator Ron Schaffner, who interviewed the of-

ficer early on. Shockey returned to the scene with fellow officer Mark Matthews later that morning in order to look for
more clues. They managed to locate some scrape marks leading down to the river.

Almost two weeks later on the evening of March 14, Officer
Matthews had a nearly identical experience. Driving down the
same thoroughfare, he spotted something in the road ahead
that appeared to be an animal carcass. Matthews brought his
vehicle to a halt and opened his car door, fully expecting to
have to collect the object. The sound of the car door opening
apparently prompted the critter to rise up into a crouched position similar to a defensive lineman and "half hobble" toward
the guardrail. This time it kept its eyes on the policeman while
it lifted its leg over the barrier, and it seemed to have an odd
smirk on its face that, according to accounts, inspired Matthews to draw his weapon and fire upon the thing. During
an interview years later, he attempted to defend this action by
suggesting that he was merely attempting to collect evidence
that would vindicate his colleague. In any event, he must have
missed, since the animal escaped into the river.

As word of the Loveland Frog spread, some dubious stories
surfaced. That May a teenager claimed that he saw a green-
skinned creature that was almost four feet long. The youth
guessed that it had weighed about 150 pounds. And before the
end of the year, a local farmer alleged that he had run across
four of the small beings while working in his field, describing
them as looking grayish-green with a toothy grin. Staying true
to form, the entities evidently vanished into the Little Miami
River once again. Things settled down after that. A vague ref-

erence from 1985 mentions two boys spotting a dog-sized frog by the river.

Overall, accounts seem to be as elusive as the cryptid itself. On a popular blog site, an anonymous person mentioned that they had seen a "big frog head with fur" sticking out of the Ohio River near Rising Sun, Indiana. A Loveland resident wrote to researcher Lon Strickler in 2011, claiming that an inhuman trespasser on her property was making noises and peering in her windows with glowing eyes at night. Since some of her windows were apparently ten feet off the ground, it's difficult to relate it to the dwarfish frogman, though Ohio does produce a marked amount of Bigfoot sightings. Returning to the 1955 account, Ted Bloecher had uncovered the following account of a potentially kindred event at the time:

> Mrs. Emily Magnone and her husband, awakened by their dog's barking, smelt a strong odor "like swamp." Their next-door neighbor went out to investigate [and] saw, 15 feet away, a 3-foot little man "entirely covered with twigs or foliage." Whenever she turned on the porch light the little man disappeared, but would reappear in the same place when it was turned off.

It should be clear why officers Shockey and Matthews were reluctant to reveal their identities following their encounters in 1972, and when they eventually did, they were apparently ridiculed to the extent that they simply didn't want to talk about it anymore. When the men finally broke their silence during the 1990s, they dropped a bombshell, stating that the animal that they had both seen in 1972 had been nothing more than an escaped pet iguana and that the whole affair had been blown entirely out of proportion. Yet one has to wonder why the initial sketch of the creature, drawn by Ray Shockey's sister and presumably under their direction, clearly depicts a bipedal, man-like, frog monster.

Furthermore, the fact that both sightings took place on frigid winter evenings when the road conditions were apparently "icy" argues against the iguana explanation. No reptile would have been active in those conditions. We have to wonder if perhaps Shockey and Matthews were simply anxious to put the whole matter to rest and felt the iguana story was the best way to accomplish that. On the website *Cryptozoology.com,* a contributor who claimed to be a lifelong Loveland resident and writer explained how his extensive foray into the mystery revealed that the 1972 sightings had all been an elaborate hoax perpetrated by the practical-joking mayor of Loveland at the time. And that he had accomplished the illusion using plastic sheets and a system of pulleys. Personally, I am not convinced that this is feasible.

At time of writing, it is uncertain if an amphibious hominid actually inhabits the Little Miami River near Loveland, though its legacy is still going strong. In 2014, a musical based on the creature made its glorious debut.

China's Titanic Toads

A number of Internet websites pay tribute to a narrative that describes a heretofore unfamiliar brood of tremendous toads that inhabit cavernous pools in China's western Hubei Province. This stems from a nebulous tale of an encounter that was supposed to have transpired during the summer of 1987. The incident allegedly involved a party of nine biologists hailing from Peking University who were conducting field research in wilderness areas close to the city of Wuhan. The operation was apparently being overseen by accomplished professor Chen Mok Chun. As the academics assembled some photographic equipment adjacent to a small lake, a trio of colossal creatures ascended from the depths of the water straight in front of them. The mystifying six-foot-wide animals resembled amphibians and had pasty, pale skin; huge eyes; and gaping mouths. After a few anxious minutes, things got really weird when one of the monsters unfurled an expanded tongue, enveloping an entire camera rig. As this unreal scene was materializing, the two other beasts belched weird and sinister shrieking sounds. In an instant, all three of the things had plunged back into the abysmal darkness of the lake and were not seen again. In the aftermath of the traumatic confrontation, one of the witnesses is said to have gotten violently ill and vomited.

Like frogs, their fellow anurans, toads are not known to have gotten close to the dimensions that were mentioned by the Chinese scientists (even in prehistoric times), and it should also be noted that the only other account we have on record is equally as ambiguous. There is a vague reference circulating online that indicates local fishermen attempted to exterminate the troublesome toads back in 1962 by hurling dynamite into the creatures' watery domain. It is said that the result of this action was that a highly territorial toad known as "Chan" chased the fishermen some thirty yards back onto dry land. Although these accounts display the earmarks of gross embellishments, the 1987 affair was reported in newspapers throughout China and was subsequently picked up by news outlets in Australia and the United States. Before completely dismissing the possibility of car-sized amphibians in China, it should be acknowledged that several new animal species have been documented in that part of the world over the past decades.

Silver Lake, Massachusetts,
is reputedly home to a monstrous frog.

Search at Silver Lake

My sole cryptic amphibian investigation transpired in October 2009 when I resolved to spend a weekend in Massachusetts while my close friend Nick Redfern, a well-known author and researcher, gave a lecture in Boston. About thirty-five miles southeast of Boston rests Silver Lake, a shallow, 640-acre body of water in Plymouth County. During the 1940s and 1950s, there apparently were stories of a macabre water monster described as either a giant frog or "small frog-man" dwelling within its depths, so, I reasoned, what better way to get to the bottom of the allegations than by going and taking a look for myself?

Following an uneventful drive down in my rental car, I located the spot. Surprisingly, it was a densely populated area with many homes bordering the lake's delightful shores. In addition, there were a few businesses along Highway 27 on its north end. I planned to hike around its entirety and inspect its serene shores as closely as possible. It was obvious that I would have to adjust my course a little at times in order to avoid trespassing on private property. Almost immediately I came upon a marshy area teeming with water lilies and a multitude of aquatic reeds protruding from the shallows—a perfect place for sizable amphibians, I thought. Forging on for at least an hour or so, I found myself at a public park that included a fishing pier. The place was strangely abandoned, given that the weather was fairly mild. I decided to engage a solitary man fishing from the dock.

We made angler small talk, and he indicated that he frequented the spot on a regular basis, primarily landing a handful of decent-sized bluegills. It was then that I dropped the million-dollar question.

"I understand that there have been reports of something like a giant frog in the lake. Ever hear of anything like that?"

The man admitted that he had never heard of such a thing, but speculated that "there could be some big catfish living in there."

As I headed back to my car defeated, I considered knocking on a few doors along the way but didn't want to risk intruding on a quiet Sunday, particularly when my sole intention was to discuss frogs of impossible dimensions hopping through their backyards. I would have liked to enter a few businesses in order to feel things out, but everything around seemed to be closed down that day.

As I strolled back to my car feeling rather frustrated, I pondered how the accounts of a monster frog in the lake could have possibly come about. The largest species of native bullfrog (*Rana catesbeiana*) only weighs a couple of pounds, hardly the makings of a legendary beast. Besides, Silver Lake is a relatively small, 640-acre body of water. Its shoreline, as I discovered, is densely populated and highly developed—not the sort of place where a sizeable animal could remain hidden. The case remains open.

Chapter 8
CREEPY-CRAWLIES

Ninety-five percent of the documented species in the animal kingdom are invertebrates—creatures without backbones that swim, slither, crawl, or fly throughout the planet's diverse environments. For the most part, we humans have an extreme unease when it comes to these assorted bugaboos. A centipede or cockroach crawling across the bathroom wall sends an intense shiver down our spines, and the tiniest spider can sometimes cause a burly man to shriek like a little girl. This aversion becomes readily understandable when we ponder the strangely alien nature of these creatures. Take for example the bloodsucking leech, a slimy, inky, little vampire that lurks in the swamp, waiting patiently to latch onto an unsuspecting victim. Then consider the disgusting and lowly maggot, which nestles itself lovingly amidst putrid, decaying flesh. Or even the sinister scorpion, which stealthily slinks across the bedroom floor prior to inflicting its deadly, venomous sting.

While most invertebrates seem tiny in comparison to humans, there are most definitely exceptions to this rule. Because some of these life-forms do not have the restrictions of a bony, internal skeleton, their growth potential is not limited. For example, squids in the deep ocean are capable of reaching gargantuan proportions. During the time that I camped along the Amazon River, I encountered ants that were an inch and a half long, cockroaches over twice that size, snails as big as my fist, and tarantulas as large as a dinner plate. In the jungles of Borneo, a species of walking stick insect (*Phobaeticus chani*) possesses a body two feet long. The Japanese spider crab (*Macrocheira kaempferi*), the world's largest known arthropod, boasts long, spindly legs that can stretch a dozen feet in length. The largest known invertebrate, the colossal squid (*Mesonychoteuthis hamiltoni*), can reach lengths of forty-six feet and can weigh over half a ton, but because it lives deep in the ocean, it was completely unknown to science until 1925.

Like most animals, invertebrates grew even larger in prehistoric times. An order of dragonfly-like insects from the Paleozoic Era had a wingspan of three feet across. They were the size of modern crows. Some of the ancient sea scorpions called eurypterids grew to over eight feet in length. Mollusks, specifically cephalopods, may have once grown to inconceivable dimensions. Because these creatures are primarily composed of soft tissues, they do not necessarily make good candidates for fossilization, so we would have no inkling if such monsters had even ever existed. Furthermore, when contemplating the deep ocean trenches, unexplored cave systems, and impenetrable jungles and swamps of the world, it is not impossible that some abominations remain undiscovered.

Georgia's Gigantic Spider

It would be difficult to list a life-form that is more maligned and feared than the spider. This is quite understandable when we consider that we are talking about creatures possessing an external skeleton, eight legs, four sets of eyes, and in some cases a fatal, venomous bite. Some strategically spin immense, sticky webs that we can stumble into face-first. Regardless, spiders are one of the most successful orders on the planet with some 40,000 species efficiently inhabiting virtually every terrain imaginable for some 300 million years now. And while most would argue that any spider is too big, the largest South American tarantula, commonly called the Goliath birdeater (*Theraphosa blondi*), boasts a leg span of about a foot and can weigh over six ounces. As its name suggests, this stout arachnid has been known to take down birds and even small mammals on occasion. By comparison, one of the largest known North American species, the Carolina wolf spider (*Hogna carolinensis*) is barely an inch long.

Accounts of monstrous spiders are rare, so I was admittedly shocked when I was contacted by a man from College Park, Georgia, who described an encounter with a nightmare-sized specimen. The witness, Christopher Williams, has an impressive background, having worked as a fireman and EMT for the past fifteen years. As Williams tells it, he was mowing his grass early one summer morning a few years ago, and when he bumped his lawnmower into the side of a tall pine tree in his front yard, the impact caused something to move. Out of the corner of his eye, Williams detected something that was brown in color easing slowly up the tree. As he turned to look, he was horrified to realize that the object in question was in fact the father of all wolf spiders and in his own words was at least eleven inches long, "as big as a house cat."

Immediately aware that he was looking at something that wasn't supposed to exist, Williams backed up slowly and headed into the house in order to retrieve either his camera or cell phone. He was admittedly concerned that such a move could place him in danger, as it might motivate the enormous arachnid to pounce on him. By the time Williams returned a couple of minutes later with camera in hand, the thing had disappeared. All I can add to this perplexing mystery is that, despite the extraordinary nature of his claim, over the phone Williams came off as an impressively sincere and credible eyewitness.

Now, while there have been some intriguing accounts of gargantuan spiders from the largely inaccessible jungles of the Congo, Papua New Guinea, and South America's Amazon basin, it is hard to imagine that an unknown arachnid of immense size could exist anywhere in temperate, suburban North America. There is one report from Leesville, Louisiana, circa 1948, when a man named William Slaydon, along with his wife Pearl and three grandsons, supposedly observed a black, washtub-sized spider emerge from the brush while they were all walking to church one evening. This particular incident came to light via Slaydon's great-grandson, documentary filmmaker Todd Partain.

In a related thread on the website *Cryptomundo*, a reader posted that they had twice witnessed foot-long spiders in eastern Iowa and that these arachnids were very rare and typically appeared in garages and barns. On yet another cryptozoology site, a woman referring to herself as "Lady Green Eyes" chimed in with this:

> [Where] my oldest was living out in Land O' Lakes FL, they had a real problem with wolf spiders. [She saw] some big ones, and she kept telling me that there was a HUGE one that hid in this one corner. You could hear it, but I thought she was exaggerating until it came up the wall one day. This sucker was as big as a sandwich plate (like the Corelle kind, in between the dinner plates and the bread-n-butter dishes)! Never heard of a wolf spider that big. Tossed a board at it, and I know I hit the thing, and I swear it must have bounced off.

A more dubious spider story appeared on a less credible website during December of 2013. An anonymous man in Lexington, Missouri, alleged that he spotted a five-foot arachnid while he was out fishing.

Despite these intriguing stories, readers with arachnophobia will be relieved to hear that according to biomechanical laws, there are extreme physiological limitations on a spider's size. For one thing, rather than lungs, arthropods utilize something known as a tracheal respiratory system in order to breathe. This arrangement relies on a complex system of tube-like structures to absorb and disperse oxygen to the cells. If a specimen were to become gigantic, such a respiratory system frankly wouldn't be efficient enough to support it. Similarly, arachnids' circulatory systems may have size restrictions, and monster-sized ones would be vulnerable to desiccation (drying out). Finally, since spiders utilize an exoskeleton, there are mobility issues that arise as their theoretical mass increases. Their muscles literally would not be able to support the weights of their heavy bodies. Taking all of this into account, we can never completely discount the miraculous force that is evolution. Provided that nature has found a way to overcome these functional obstacles, the super spiders are not a total impossibility.

Meg Buick's interpretation
of Georgia's Giant Spider.

She's Got Legs: Colossal Centipedes of the Ozarks

If the notion of spiders the size of frying pans is not enough to make you check under your sheets, imagine an elongate, multilegged creature over a foot long and capable of inflicting an excruciating, venomous sting by way of its two, huge mandibles. Now picture the thing crawling out of a hollow tree trunk right in the middle of the American heartland! Like spiders, centipedes are segmented arthropods. However, they belong to a completely different subphylum with a lineage dating back some 400 million years to the Silurian Period. Most, of course, are tiny. But the largest specimens of the genus *Scolopendra* can grow to be twelve inches in length and an inch wide, though these are only found in the tropical jungles of South America and the Caribbean. One species that is native to parts of North America (*Scolopendra heros*) is known to top out at around seven inches, though there are accounts that indicate something twice as large.

Silas "Claib" Claiborne Turnbo was one of Arkansas's most prolific chroniclers of the late nineteenth century. Born in Taney County, Missouri, on May 26, 1844, Turnbo was the oldest of eleven children and later went on to serve in the Civil War. He was also known as a bit of an esoteric wanderer, who spoke to many residents of the Ozark Mountains throughout the course of his life, recording the colorful stories that he heard. Turnbo documented several cases where individuals allegedly came across monster-sized centipedes in the forests of southern Missouri and northern Arkansas and in one case had even preserved the specimen in a giant pickle jar.

In one instance, a hunter named R. M. Jones claimed that he shot a foot-long centipede as it was posturing to attack one of Turnbo's younger brothers at the base of a bluff. On still another occasion Clear Creek resident William Patton stated that he killed a gigantic specimen that crawled into a hollow tree near the village of Powell. After extracting the thing's carcass, Patton was able to estimate its length at fourteen inches. According to Turnbo, the grandfather of all centipedes was caught by a man with the colorful name of Bent Music at a place called Jimmies Creek in Marion County, Arkansas. When stretched out on a table and measured, it spanned an unbelievable eighteen inches. The monstrosity was placed in a large glass jar filled with alcohol and put on display in a drugstore in the town of Yellville, where Turnbo as well as many others ultimately saw it. Turnbo recalled, "It was of such unusual size that it made one almost shudder to look at it." Unfortunately, the remarkable specimen vanished during the chaos of the Civil War, and no one knows its current whereabouts.

Arkansas apparently is not the only state where these vermin are found either. In neighboring Texas, where (according to the locals) virtually everything is bigger, a newspaper article from the *Dallas Morning News* printed on April 30, 1903, chronicles a similar account: "PARIS—Conductor E.S. Lowrance of the Frisco came in on his run this morning with a monster centipede ten inches long in a big pickle jar. A fisherman at Buck Creek tank, in the Territory, made him a present of it."

While the idea of something as exceptional as a foot-long arthropod eluding the far-reaching scope of American entomologists seems unlikely, it has been estimated that there may be as many as 5,000 undocumented species of centipede.

India's Gold-Digging Ants

Considered the father of written history, the ancient Greek luminary Herodotus chronicled many events that painted a romantic picture of the Old World. While he is credited with many great accomplishments, some of his accounts are viewed as a tad whimsical. Such is the case of his so-called gold-digging ants. Writing about the sandy wastelands of India he asserts,

> Here, in this desert, there live amid the sand great ants, in size somewhat less than dogs, but bigger than foxes. The Persian king has a number of them, which have been caught by hunters in the land whereof we are speaking. Those ants make their dwellings under the ground, and

like the Greek ants, which they very much resemble in shape, throw up sand-heaps as they burrow. Now the sand which they throw up is full of gold. The Indians when they go into the desert to collect this sand take three camels and harness them together.... When the Indians therefore have equipped themselves they set off in quest of the gold, calculating the time so they may be engaged in seizing it during the most sultry part of the day, when the ants hide themselves to escape the heat.

The possibility of prospecting ants seems rather far-fetched to say the least, but the notion of them being dog-sized conjures images reminiscent of an Atomic Age Saturday matinée. Fortunately, for any Indian picnickers, there is a rational explanation. During 1996, a French ethnologist named Michel Peissel was exploring a high plateau called the Dansar plain, which overlooks the Indus River. While doing so, he spoke with many of the isolated Minaro people from both India and neighboring Pakistan, who informed him that their ancestors used to collect gold dust from sand that had been dug up by burrowing rodents called marmots (*Marmota himalayana*). Apparently, these large ground squirrels possess a local name that translates essentially to "mountain ant," no doubt due to the fact that, like their six-legged counterparts, they are fond of digging holes in the ground. It would seem that Herodotus merely made an assumption based on what he had heard from his Indian contacts, and there are likely no gold-digging arthropods in India.

A Whopper of a Wasp

Personally, I have no quarrel with the spiders, centipedes, or most other large arthropods of Earth. Generally speaking, they do not bug me much. On the other hand, place me in the flight path of an aggressive, winged insect that can either sting or bite, and you are apt to see hysterics the likes of which you've never witnessed before. True, I have been swarmed by a nest of angry hornets, had deer flies (*Chrysops*) in Canada bite me so hard that I yelled like an air horn, and had some baseball-sized "thing" (*shudders*) dive-bomb me on the Guatemalan border. But my irrational distaste and fear of flying insects dates back to my early childhood. Consequently, the following report gleaned from the Gulf Coast Bigfoot Research Organization website represents a personal hell of sorts. The writer, an anonymous Marine stationed at the Marine Corps Air Ground Combat Center in Twentynine Palms, California, during 1992 explains,

> Our Light Armored Vehicles were parked on a huge area of desert land (we called the ramp) that is either concrete or sand, several acres in size. One day while resting in the shade during lunch, several of us Marines noticed something about the size of a small dog, maybe 6 inches tall and about 18 inches long, very skinny; it was darting back and forth along the ramp, under and between the vehicles, at very high speeds, covering hundreds of yards in seconds. A few of us decided to investigate and we were amazed to find that when we got close to the thing it was a giant insect! It appeared to be a giant wasp, black and red. It was [too] long to catch with a five gallon

bucket, because believe me we tried to catch it for about an hour. It moved so fast, that you could not see if it moved at top speed at distances of about 10–30 [feet per second]. One second it would be in front of you and then it would dart away so fast you could not see it, and then it would be 15 feet to your left. It was over 18 inches long, about 6 inches tall, and its head was a little bigger than a golf ball but more football shaped. It had wings but never did fly. When running at top speeds over the sand it threw sand in the air like a boat leaves a wake. It made noises and appeared threatening. It was so intimidating that more than six Marines decided not to mess with it anymore after trying to catch it made it very mad. I've seen big insects in Africa and other places I visited while in the military, but never anything this big and ugly and mean and fast, it was truly amazing.

It is worth noting that the largest tarantula wasp species only grows to be about three inches long, so unless we are willing to concede that the military is secretly engineering a breed of super-sized wasp-weapons, there is no accounting for its estimated girth. Continuing along this line of speculation, we have an account that seemingly takes this concept to the next level.

Attack of the Mantis People!

In the 1997 science-fiction film *Mimic*, monstrous mutant insects take on the appearance of humans as the result of a genetic experiment gone awry. This scenario is highly improbable, of course. However, there are indications that something beyond diabolical is underway in the high deserts of California. My first and only clue came via e-mail from a man named Daniel, who wrote,

> My coworker John told me a story of something he had seen and had not talked about since he was in high school. He says one night when he was alone at home, he went to the front door to open it and get some fresh air. When he did so, he had a feeling come over him to look to his side. When he turned his head, he saw something on the adjacent building on the wall. It was about the size of a man. He took notice that it looked like it was armor plated, and it immediately gave him the distinct impression that it was an insect. It was dark in color. When it looked up at him, it took a few steps up the wall backwards, facing him. John says it then blended into the wall and disappeared. It scared him so much that he went inside, locked the door and closed all the blinds. Then he turned off the lights in fear that it would see him. It scared John so bad that he stayed up all night until the sun came up. He only told a few people, including his sister, his girlfriend, and me. John hasn't seen anything since, but it left that image burned in his mind.

According to Daniel, the situation got even more interesting when he heard about a seemingly corroborating encounter that involved one of his other coworkers.

> Troy's encounter came in the middle of the night when he and a friend were going to investigate an alleged haunted house. As they were pulling up to it, he turned

off his lights, and he says it was then that something jumped into the back of his truck, a raised F-150. It was so heavy it had dipped the truck, as if a 500-pound man jumped in the back of it. Troy looked to see what had happened. Then he just caught a glimpse of it jumping over to the front end of the vehicle. It landed in front of the hood, facing the truck but still hunched over. It slowly stood up. It looked armor plated and dark in color, with long, strange-looking hands or mandibles and long, animalistic hind legs, but it was bipedal. Troy said he had to bend over the steering wheel and look up out of his windshield to see the top of it. Just when he did, he says it jumped thirty to fifty feet to the side and started running. Troy tried to keep up with it in the truck and noticed it was running about thirty to sixty miles per hour, turning into a dried-up riverbed and running faster than them. Troy tried to keep pace, but he was on a dirt road. He had to stop because the road ended, and he lost sight of it.

While there is no definitive evidence that 500-pound, man-like insects actually exist, within UFO circles there are descriptions of aliens with insect-like features. Sometimes referred to as "insectoid" extraterrestrials, they are depicted as resembling the praying mantis insects of Earth, displaying an upright posture and obtaining heights of eight to nine feet. According to some experts, these beings are at the top of the extraterrestrial hierarchy and often oversee abductions and examinations of unwilling human victims. Though I'm personally not inclined to endorse such suggestions, I offer one here as a possible explanation, provided we are willing to acknowledge that we are not alone.

Missouri's Metallic Blob

I readily admit that when it comes to accounts of amorphous blob-like creatures slithering about the ground, my files are pretty scant. Consequently, I was flabbergasted to receive the following correspondence from a woman named Kourtney.

> About ten years ago, after moving into my new house in Missouri, I walked out onto the front porch. I was standing there quietly looking around. I saw something moving out of the corner of my eye. I assumed immediately it was a mouse. There on the porch was a silver mass about the size of my hand. It looked like melted silver to be truthful. Yet it moved with purpose of direction, like liquid. Moving and turning, and I swear it seemed to notice me. Then it kind of shot under and up one of the plastic porch beams. Crazy, I know. I assume it could have been a deformed animal/insect. I don't know. I've tried finding out what it could be, but nothing I've read about is similar to what I know I saw. Is this something you've ever heard of? It's totally crazy, right?

Rest assured, Kourtney—in my line of work, nothing is totally crazy. I'm constantly contacted by normal, everyday people who claim to have had experiences that go against everything we think we know about the world and universe that we live in. That said, I really am at a loss to offer an explanation for animate, terrestrial blobs without sounding like a science-fiction movie. Obviously, the oceans are teeming with an array of gelatinous life-forms well suited to living in that particular environment. I encourage any reader with a similar experience or insight to get in touch with me.

Invisible Insects?

An e-mail that I received from a man named René years ago inspired a thought-provoking abstraction. Obviously, our planet is a complex ecosystem, literally overflowing with a diverse abundance of microorganisms that make up the foundation for all life on Earth. Though these creatures surround us, we are not able to see them without the aid of a microscope. Similarly, there are species in the animal kingdom (arthropods and insects) that are so incredibly tiny that we are not easily able to perceive them, essentially qualifying them as "unknowns." Might some exceptionally diminutive types have evolved with the ability to alter how they are affected by the light spectrum, thus rendering themselves completely invisible to us? René ponders this dilemma.

> Is it possible that there are certain types of creatures ... insects ... that exist outside our visual range? I experienced something one day while visiting at my mother's house. We were outside on the patio, and it was a sunny day. I was sitting at a stone-top table and was kind of bored. So I saw some very small insects about the size of a pinhead. They were red in color, and even though I have seen them all my life, I never bothered to find out what

they were. I took a metal rod about half the size of a pen-
cil, half as long; maybe it was a type of aluminum nail. So
I crushed the bug. Or at least I thought I did. I couldn't
find its crushed carcass. So I did it again to another one
that was close by, and … same thing. After I would crush
it, the body would not be there. And now the other bugs
were gone. I couldn't see them anymore. So from this
I figured or thought—Is it possible that this insect can
change the way light reflects off its shell so that it no longer appears in our visual spectrum?

My best guess is that the insects René encountered at his
mother's house are commonly referred to as red spider mites
(*Tetranychus urticae*), which are barely visible to the naked human eye, and that his act of crushing them evacuated their
internal body contents, which are brightly colored. Since all
that remained was their transparent outer body wall, they became impossible for him to see with his naked eye. If, however, nearby mites that were fearful of being crushed by René
actually managed to turn invisible in a desperate act of self-
preservation, I'm at a loss to explain it.

Nature, in all its strange splendor, has produced specialized
animals that are capable of creating electricity and of glowing
via bioluminescence, and some are even capable of camouflag-
ing themselves relative to their surroundings by altering the
color and texture of their skin. Would it be totally unexpected
to ultimately find insects capable of going into *Predator* mode
by somehow superficially simulating invisibility? I think not.

Chapter 9
PHANTOMS, FAIRIES, AND MERMAIDS

After a considerable amount of soul-searching, I decided to include this slightly whimsical chapter, which addresses some of the spectral and otherworldly creatures I've come across during the course of my research. Admittedly, none of them deserve any consideration in terms of a possible affiliation to the natural or zoological world. Still, I offer them here not only for entertainment value but also because, in my humble opinion, the scientific process does not grant us the luxury of entirely ruling out any possibility. Who's to say what can and can't exist in our vast universe? Furthermore, contemplation, while not always resulting in definitive answers, often manages to teach us something... and it's usually about ourselves.

Those Fishy Mermaids

Within the pantheon of mythical man-beasts, those alluring sea-dwelling sirens known as mermaids harbor a sacred place in our imaginations. While the notion of a piscine enchantress rising out of the watery depths is romantic, it contradicts everything we know about the evolution of hominid forms on our planet. Though, that certainly didn't discourage one popular television network from producing two elaborate (and quite ludicrous) "documentaries" claiming to reveal never-before-seen evidence that mermaids actually do exist. While I am admittedly hesitant to endorse such a far-flung notion, at the same time I'm willing to acknowledge that anything is conceivable, particularly in the unexplored ocean depths. Furthermore, there is a measurable degree of antiquity in regard to the fishy ones. Thousands of years ago, the ancient Babylonians worshipped a deity known as *Oannes,* essentially a man-fish who would come ashore in order to impart his vast knowledge on the land dwellers. Encounters with merfolk were apparently plentiful in bygone days but have since entered the domain of popular fantasy. Fleeting modern accounts still surface on rare occasion, around every twenty years or so.

Thomas Finley's interpretation of a mermaid.

- In May of 1935, the crew of a fishing boat allegedly tried in vain to capture a ten-foot, bearded merman with glowing eyes off Redondo Beach, California.

- Sometime during World War II, a sailor named Rein Mellart claimed that he watched local fisherman on the Indonesian island of Morotai dredge up a mermaid in their nets. Mellart said he was able to observe the creature in great detail before it died on the beach while struggling in the net. He described the classic features: a female human torso with a flowing head of hair attached to a "bottom half like a dolphin." However, Mellart also noted that far from being attractive, the entity possessed coarse features, a long nose, and two thumbs per hand.

- In August of 1949, local fishermen alleged mermaid sightings off Craigmore, Scotland.

- On a stormy night in November of 1958 at Mecklenburg Bay, Germany, two men aboard a fishing trawler claimed they were saved from certain disaster by a man-fish with green seaweed hair, who rose from the depths and guided them to safe anchorage.

- In 1962, an Italian magazine called *La Domenica del Corriere* published a story about a fisherman named Colmaro Orsini who alleged that he heard a beautiful song and looked up just in time to see a woman with green hair and a fish tail rising from the sea.

- During 1967, ferry passengers at Active Pass, British Columbia, Canada, supposedly watched a blonde-haired mermaid while she sat on a rock, eating a salmon. Though there were claims of a photo taken, as we might expect, details and sources are ambiguous.

- In perhaps the most dramatic encounter, during 1988 an Australian diver named Robert Froster reported to a Florida newspaper that while diving a few miles off Florida's Gulf Coast, he was accosted by an exceptionally irate mermaid who chased him all the way to the surface. Froster characterized the creature as having long, flowing hair, smooth skin with human breasts and a scaly fish's tail.

• Surprisingly there is even a spate of twenty-first-century sightings originating in the coastal city of Kiryat Yam, Israel. In August or September of 2009, a witness stated that he came upon a strange-looking woman writhing around on the sandy beach. In an instant, the being disappeared into the surf, displaying the fluidity of a native marine specimen. Other rumored incidents soon followed.

Despite the fact that mermaids could regularly be found in natural history guides mere centuries ago, it is now generally accepted that these accounts were based on encounters with real animals, such as dugongs, manatees, seals, sea lions, and walruses. From a distance, all of these marine mammals are capable of displaying quasi-humanlike features. It's not hard to conceive that sailors on long and largely uneventful voyages would glimpse these round-headed beasts rising out of the surf ever so briefly on the horizon and let their fanciful imaginations take over. Or just maybe, deep below the surface in some inconceivable underwater kingdom, a race of fabulous merbeings reign supreme. Personally, I won't hold my breath.

The Winged Ones

The airborne counterparts of mermaids are the myriad of flying humanoids that I explored in my previous book, *Encounters with Flying Humanoids: Mothman, Man Birds, Gargoyles*

& Other Winged Beasts. Apart from West Virginia's famous Mothman, England's macabre Owlman, and the Houston Batman are two of the more familiar creatures of this order. It is an utterly perplexing phenomenon to be sure, and presumably with more of a connection to the supernatural as opposed to the corporeal—they are definitely not flesh-and-blood creatures. Since that book's publication, I have received a handful of relevant accounts from seemingly sincere people.

One of the more extraordinary sightings I've heard of was related to me by a man named Trey. One moonlit evening during September of 2012, Trey and his wife were sitting outside their home in Big Spring, Texas, which is located in the extreme western part of the state. Their property is situated near a state park in a semiarid region peppered with many hills and mesas. That particular night, the couple was watching a storm that was brewing in the distance. At some point they both noticed something in the faraway sky approaching them silently. As the mysterious object came closer, it descended until it was only about thirty feet above their heads, at which point it became evident that the apparition was some type of winged man of giant proportions. The being eerily turned its head and looked directly at them as he flew over.

According to Trey, the entity appeared human, having long, flowing hair; slanted, solid black eyes; a powerful jaw; and slight nose with long nostrils. Moreover, in his estimation the apparition was a gray color, had a twenty-foot wingspan, and would have stood anywhere from ten to fourteen feet tall. Trey was also able to make out some other specific details. In addition to angelic, feathered wings, the figure had long arms that it held tightly against its body and what appeared to be normal-looking hands, though its feet had exaggerated arches. Interestingly, the humanoid did not appear to possess nipples, genitalia, or even a belly button, though its rib cage was prominent. The subject flew on for a few blocks until it was out of their sight.

Also in Texas, there was another disturbing encounter from roughly the same time period. I was contacted by a young woman who seemed understandably distressed by the entire affair and prefers to remain anonymous.

I live in the southeast side of Houston, in the North Shore/Cloverleaf area. I was waiting for my husband to get home … because he was running late that night. My dog and I went on the back porch … Initially my dog was barking with his hair raised, but I thought he [had] just smelled or seen a coon or possum. … When to shock and awe I looked up as a huge, man/bat thing swooped in at me. Its feet were about five to six feet from my head. I had my porch light on, but it was so massive it still cast a shadow over me and the lawn as it went away. It literally blacked out the sky beneath it. I felt animosity from it. My initial thought was it was trying to seize me or the dog up, so I … went inside my house. I am not crazy. It had skin not feathers. It looked extremely built or muscular but lean. … Needless to say, I am shaken by this. I don't want to be ridiculed. I do not have hallucinations. I don't do drugs or drink. This was as real as it gets … I know the area where I live has plenty of water and stray dogs. I lived out in the country for eight years and never was scared or seen/experienced anything like this. . . . It looked as if it could take on a big dog or a child . . . This is very dangerous.

During the course of follow-up correspondence with this young woman, she confided that a couple of nights after the incident she thought she heard something quite large landing in a tree in her front yard. Whatever it was had broken several large, dead tree limbs. It seems that these kinds of experiences often have lingering effects. Generally speaking, the flying humanoid problem is one that is very difficult to wrap one's head around. Like mermaids, they simply should not exist. Furthermore, it seems there is no place that is immune to the strangeness, as evidenced by the following e-mail I received from a man living in the town of Richmond, Indiana. At the time of his encounter, he was driving home in the evening and along a deserted country road, as you might guess.

About one-third of the way down the dark road, I stuck my head out to have my face in the wind as I usually did . . . [and] looked up at the moon and pretty stars. I pulled my head in, and that's when I heard a *woosh* sound . . . go by outside. It sounded like a big bird or something. . . . I thought *owl*, but kept driving as usual. Then something *wooshed* right in from of my car [through] the headlights, super fast. It took me aback because it was big. . . . I mean it seemed like the whole length of the front of the car or more. At that point I knew something was not right or different. I remember thinking, I just wanna get off this road and home. All the way down the road I heard weird noises and *woosh*es. I was thinking bats and birds and such don't do this and follow you, because this thing was following me down the road.... So I floored the car and made it to the end of the road and around the bend where I saw some city edge lights.... Now I was in town and there were lights, so I looked out my window... [and saw] against the moon... a huge dark silhouette with flapping, bat-like wings.... I mean a wingspan of like seven to nine feet from tip to tip... and humanoid feet hanging down a bit.... My heart was pounding.... I couldn't believe what I was seeing... so I just gassed it and got home.

Due to the often brief and heart-pounding nature of these kinds of encounters, we are usually left with only the faintest of descriptions. A curious secondhand account materialized on the popular cryptozoology website *Cryptomundo* following one of my appearances on the nationally syndicated radio show, *Coast to Coast AM*. The contributor's name was William Myrkle, and he wrote,

My friend whom I had not seen in years recently told me about a black glowing thing that she has seen on two occasions. She saw it flying through the trees at the edge of the woods behind her house, about 10 feet or so off the ground. She didn't recall seeing a head or wings, as she could only get glimpses of it through the trees as it passed by. She did note that the hind legs were very muscular and looked like that of a horse. She said that every dog in the neighborhood was barking, and her cats were also very aware of it, and quite startled. She had asked a neighbor if he had ever seen anything out of the ordinary, without telling him what she had seen, and he came back with, "Oh, you mean the glowing thing?"

Perhaps I am taking a bit of a leap by including this episode here, particularly in lieu of a more detailed description. However, I believe the characterization of the anomaly's legs as looking "muscular" eliminates any possibility of bird or bat, not to mention the fact that the thing glowed! As far as the meaning behind all of it, I leave that for you to make sense of, my dear reader.

The following is a slightly more tangible report, though it's frustratingly brief.

The sighting was related to me by Utah resident Karen, who was working a trucking route with her husband from California to Nevada during 2007 to 2008. The couple was motoring up I-15 North around 8:00 or 9:00 p.m. one night. Without warning, some "thing with wings" landed briefly in the road ahead of them and then took off again quickly, as if sensing their truck barreling down on it. What struck Karen was that the creature was big—at least as tall as man, about six feet high or so, with a ten-foot wingspan—and that its hide was gray, leathery, and devoid of feathers. Its wings appeared bat-like and membranous. But the aspect that is really ingrained in Karen's memory is the fact that the apparition displayed long, manlike legs, a clear indicator that this was no animal. In retrospect, she also felt as if the thing may have exuded a level of intelligence, based on its strategic movements.

Bayou Cyclops

One of the strangest creatures' chronicles that I've ever come across involves a monstrous brute that seems to have stepped right out of Greek mythology and squarely into a swampy Louisiana parish. In my line of work, this juncture shouldn't come as a total shock, since I've investigated contemporary accounts of other epic villains likened to satyrs and harpies, yet this narrative truly stands alone. The details come courtesy of the Gulf Coast Bigfoot Research Organization, which posts reports of weird encounters on their website. The event allegedly occurred near a wooded area around 9:00 p.m. one evening back in November of 1957. The identity of the author is not disclosed.

Three friends and I had been to a movie and dinner and were driving around talking. As we crossed the Tangipahoa River Bridge and were approaching the small bridge immediately after, we all saw someone walking up out of the ditch on the passenger side of the car. The height of this person made me think "GIANT." We drove to the next available spot in order to turn around and go back and when we returned this person was still standing on the side of the road. We angled our car to make full use of the headlights and stopped in the road. This guy had to be every bit of 7½ feet tall and was pretty hefty. I'd say around 325 pounds. He appeared to be wearing a pair of pants and shirt that was very dark (bluish) in color and very tattered. We didn't notice if he wore any shoes.

The most horrifying feature was the shape of his nose, which resembled a snout and instead of having two eyes, there was only one located off-center on his forehead. After a minute or two this guy turned and walked back down the incline into the woods and we sped away. When we reached the nearest town we went to the police and reported our sighting but were only scoffed away. My three friends and I have often discussed this night and our only conclusion is that it was a malformed person that had been kept locked up somewhere that had escaped. All four of us lived no more than 5 miles of this sighting and have never heard anyone else talk about it.

I must confess that cyclopean confrontations are exceptionally uncommon, as far as I know, though I am aware of a situation in 1966 when a couple in Newport, Oregon, reported to police that they spotted a group of cyclops-like entities leering at them. There are, I think, a couple of intriguing circumstances that could shed some light the origins of the cyclops in Greek mythology, one component being the discovery of pygmy mastodon skulls on Mediterranean islands. Elephant skulls bare a superficial similarity to human skulls due to a large frontal cranium, and the giant nasal cavity smack dab in the middle somewhat resembles a singular eye socket. It's not hard to imagine ancient people postulating a one-eyed giant in order to explain these finds. There is also a rare genetic defect known as cyclocephaly, whereby the two orbits of a developing fetus ultimately merge and become one large eye. These genetic aberrations are typically stillborn, but on rare occasions they do manage to live for brief periods. Imagine the type of impact that animals and even humans born with one great eye would have had on people during ancient times.

Present-Day Fairy Tales

All over the world there are tales of magical, forest-dwelling beings who wreak mischief upon the world of mortals. Throughout the folklore of Western Europe, we hear references to an entire hierarchy of fairies, elves, pixies, gnomes, goblins, trolls, leprechauns, gremlins, and a host of other entities that exist in a mist-shrouded realm, where a veil of mysticism obscures their true nature. In other cultures, the vernacular is different, though the stories of little folk are familiar. It might surprise you to learn that accounts of these occult apparitions are not always relegated to dusty books and fairy tales. I offer these contemporary reports with no prejudice … and certainly no plausible explanation.

- Sometime during the 1960s, a resident of Victoria Road in Colchester, Essex, England, claimed that he watched a group of fairies dancing around an old tree trunk.
- On October 4, 1965, three panicked schoolchildren entered the headmaster's office at the Liberator General San Martin School in Salta, Argentina, stating that they had been attacked by a gaggle of green, dwarflike beings.
- On October 29, 1979, in Wollaton Park, Nottingham, England, around dusk a group of eight- to ten-year-old children heard a bell ringing. When they went to investigate, they allegedly saw sixty tiny gnomes in a swampy area. The diminutive beings had wrinkled skin and long, white beards. They wore blue shirts, yellow tights, and floppy, red hats.

According to the children, the figures were driving around in thirty little, magic bubble cars (two gnomes per car).

• In 1982 at Jaywick, near Clacton-on-Sea, Essex, two girls supposedly watched a pair of gnomes digging a hole in the playground of the Frobisher Primary School.

• During 1990, a resident of the village of Ashby-de-la-Zouch in Leicestershire awoke in the middle of the night and encountered what she believed to be an entity known as a pooka, sleeping over the pelmet of a landing window. The creature looked similar to a small piglet, but had a long, pointy nose and no visible tail.

• As recently as March of 2008, several teenage boys from General Güemes, Salta Province, Argentina, videotaped a short, gnomelike figure as it side-shuffled out of some tall weeds. Just prior to its appearance, the young men had heard sounds like stones being thrown in their direction. One of the youths was so traumatized by the incident that he had to be taken to the hospital. Witness José Alvarez stated that other locals had approached him later on and told him that they had also seen the macabre little being.

Hat Man

As an investigator of anomalous phenomena, I am often provided not-of-this-world scenarios that are very much on the fringe of what we perceive to be reality. I always tell those armed with a cosmic view that I am a "flesh-and-blood" guy, meaning that I am in my comfort zone while pursuing physical evidence, as opposed to contemplating highly subjective spectral claims. That said, due to the nature of my research, I am often approached by people who are desperate to find answers for inexplicable things they have experienced in their lives. Furthermore, it's a common notion that ambiguous relationships may exist between seemingly unrelated types of phenomena, including Bigfoot, UFOs, ghosts, and the like. In truth, who can say if some of these enigmas may truly overlap? There is so much that our neural hardware cannot fathom. One example is the very strange saga of the nefarious phantom known as the Hat Man, said to be a "shadow person" that manifests out of the darkness, spooking his victims. A typical encounter was related to me by a San Antonio resident named Jessica.

I have seen weird shadows and figures of absolute darkness most of my life. However, not since 2007 have I witnessed any shadow beings. I always manage to ignore them by rolling over and going back to sleep— completely unafraid. I am now pregnant and last Saturday night woke up in the middle of the night feeling that someone was watching me. I rolled over and saw a man standing in my bathroom doorway. I wanted to scream but was halted by the sight of the figure. He was extremely tall [and] solid black, blacker than the darkest black you can imagine. A black that is devoid of any light or color. His outfit appeared to be a trench coat of some sort but I was more focused on his face. His face glowed faintly pale blue/white, and [it] was slightly turned to the side and was looking down, yet still at me. He was wearing a black top hat. I had this horrible feeling he wanted my child. It was as if he couldn't tell if I were awake or asleep and moved back then forward, then back, then forward, until I lifted my head and blinked—[then] he was gone. I tried to recreate what I saw by closing my eyes for a long time, opening them and looking for reflections of light, etc. But I could just easily see the bathroom walls and floor, when a few minutes before I could only see blackness. I haven't seen him since then, but now I sleep with the lights on ... I am terrified!

Yet another creepy and disturbing encounter with the Hat Man involved a woman named Stacy Alejos. According to Alejos, when she was a very young girl living on the far west side of San Antonio, she was awakened one night by an uncomfortable sensation and felt eerily compelled to look out her bedroom window. As her eyes adjusted to the darkness, Alejos could clearly make out the outline of a manlike figure standing just behind the white picket fence that surrounded her yard. Though she couldn't see much in the way of features, she could clearly discern what she interpreted to be a pork pie hat atop the dark figure's head. As she watched fearfully, the being began to sidle in a strange sideways motion, all the while keeping his outstretched arms on the top fence.

When she heard the audible crunching of dried leaves beneath the entity's feet, Alejos became convinced that she was not dreaming nor imagining things. Strangely, all attempts to wake up her aunt who was sleeping in the bed next to her were futile, as if the woman was in a trancelike state. Understandably terrified, the young girl dove beneath her sheets, trembling in fear until the morning. Of possible relevance is the fact that her parents had once claimed to have seen a disk-shaped UFO hovering above their property, potentially indicating a so-called window area (where strange things occur). Admittedly, Alejos later developed an interest in paranormal topics, including experimentation with Ouija boards. Without a doubt, some will perceive this as further evidence that an amorphous connection exists between all aspects of the metaphysical.

Hat Man encounters seem to be quite common, a fact that can be substantiated with minimal Internet research. Because many of the experiences seem to occur in the twilight state of consciousness when people are waking from sleep, it has been suggested that these episodes are merely a form of night terrors, essentially frightening hallucinations that the human mind is apt to construct when in a vulnerable, dreamlike state. For deep-rooted psychological reasons, the image of a tall, mysterious man draped in a trench coat and hat may be irresistible to us. However, for those who have seen him, the Hat Man is very scary and real, and it would be difficult to convince them otherwise.

Black-Eyed Children

Equally as spooky as the Hat Man are the spectral entities referred to as the Black-Eyed Children or Black-Eyed Kids (BEKs), which have only become fashionable over the past few years as a result of popularization on offbeat Internet sites. Granted there is every reason to believe that like their Internet counterpart, Slender Man, most of the stories can be chalked up to flights of fancy meant to inspire goose bumps. At the same time, experiences like those of truck driver John Jackson cause us to wonder.

Sam Shearon's interpretation of the Black-Eyed Children.

Jackson was a black top veteran, having made long hauls for the past thirty-three years. He also came across as a no nonsense kind of guy who was going to call them as he saw them and admittedly had seen a lot of peculiar sights while making his countless cross-country runs. During April of 2015, Jackson had a troubling encounter that topped them all. It was between 1:00 and 3:00 a.m., and it was a soggy night; a sort of mist was swirling that teetered on developing into light rain. He was motoring east on Texas Highway 29, between the towns of Menard and Mason. This is an exceptionally desolate stretch of road surrounded by wide, open, scrubby ranch land sparsely dotted with homes and businesses. Suddenly, Jackson noticed what appeared to be three young people ambling towards him on the side of the road. He began to brake and wondered who in blazes would be out walking around in those conditions. Perhaps they were having car trouble, he reasoned.

As he got closer to the three figures, Jackson began to feel an uneasiness that quickly made his skin crawl. The beings were all wearing matching uniforms composed of dark-colored hoodies and were walking with their heads down, as if staring at the road in front of them. His gut was telling him that there was something really odd about the situation: "Something just didn't feel right." As he slowed to pass the figures, his suspicions were realized when one of the youngsters looked up at the very last second and pointed directly at him. It was then (in the glow of his side LEDs) that he noticed the apparition's skin was a pale white hue similar to an albino's and that its eyes were solid black. The ensuing chill that ran down Jackson's spine convinced him to put his pedal to the metal and speed off.

Never having investigated a case involving the so-called Black-Eyed Children, I was not really sure what to think. Imagine my surprise when a quick scan of the Internet revealed that all of the components that Jackson had mentioned—a remote area, hitchhiking behavior, hoodies, pale skin, and, of course, those utterly perplexing peepers—were tantamount to the quintessential BEK encounter. Furthermore, the location is only one hundred miles due south of the city of Abilene, which is credited with the most notable BEK sighting to date. My interview with Jackson revealed that he was completely unaware of the BEK phenomenon and moreover had absolutely no interest in the unexplained or anything strange whatsoever. He had simply seen something that had frightened him despite a lifetime of experience, something that he could find no explanation for. Admittedly, I haven't found one either.

Strangely and tragically, I was recently informed by a mutual friend that Jackson passed away quite suddenly just a few months after he and I spoke about his unsettling experience…and at time of writing, the cause of his death is somewhat shrouded in mystery. Could his BEK encounter have served as some kind of ominous warning? We may never know. At times, there appear to be things in this world that we're incapable of fully understanding.

CONCLUSION

At last we've reached the end of our menagerie tour. I hope you've been at the very least amused by these tantalizing tales of cryptid creatures and fabulous beasts. For those who find it difficult to give even a shred of credibility to these stories due to the microchip era that we live in, I offer you some things to ponder. Despite remarkable developments in technology, our planet is still vast and largely unexplored. Around three-quarters of the Earth is covered by an extremely deep-water environment that we know virtually nothing about. About half of the remaining land is wilderness area, essentially un-touched by man. Consider all of the impassable mountain ranges, sprawling jungles and forests, remote swamps and des-erts, and, not to mention, the expansive tundra. The potential for discovery is immense, and, indeed, discoveries have been made. In the last century, many megafauna animals including the colossal squid (confirmed in 1925), kouprey (1937), mega-mouth shark (1976), Vu Quang ox (1993), giant muntjac (1994), Perrin's beaked whale (2002), and Kabomani tapir (2013) have been formally described by scientists. We still haven't documented everything that is out there.

So the very next time you are walking alone along the edge of the twilight forest and something just out of sight begins to move, causing the brush to pop and crack, remember that it wasn't all that long ago that our ancestors huddled around a fire in the darkness of night, anxiously whispering about a myriad of rare but monstrous creatures that one hopes to never encounter ... The world is not such a different place today.

ACKNOWLEDGMENTS

I should like to take the opportunity to express my thanks to the following people, without whom this book would not have been possible: my bright, hardworking, and adventurous family; my loving and supportive girlfriend, Jen Devillier; Sydney Colvin of *Cryptid Chronicles*, who coordinated the interior illustrations and photos; and everyone at Llewellyn for providing a most enjoyable work environment.

I am especially indebted to a number of respected colleagues and friends whose tireless and passionate research continually serves to inspire me. They include Nick Redfern, Lee Hales, Lyle Blackburn, Jon Downes, Richard Freeman, Dr. Karl P.N. Shuker, John Kirk, Adam Davies, Craig Woolheater, Chester Moore, Bobby Hamilton, Scott Marlowe, Linda Godfrey, Stan Gordon, Loren Coleman, Mark Hall, Nick Sucik, Ben Radford, Matt Bille, Chad Arment, J. Robert Alley, Steve Kulls, Scott Mardis, and Paul Nation.

Thanks are also due to the pioneering fathers of my discipline, most of whom I never had the distinct honor of meeting.

They include Dr. Bernard Heuvelmans, Ivan T. Sanderson, Dr. Grover S. Krantz, Dr. Roy P. Mackal, Lt. Cdr. Rupert T. Gould, Wille Ley, Ralph Izzard, Tom Slick, Tim Dinsdale, John Keel, F. W. Holiday, John Green, Rene Dahinden, Richard Greenwell, and Jean-Jacques Barloy.

I obviously owe a huge debt of gratitude to the many courageous eyewitnesses who kindly granted me permission to share their remarkable stories. Finally, I'd like to acknowledge you, the reader, for being curious enough to explore these pages.

BIBLIOGRAPHY

Anonymous eyewitness. "Report #6463." Bigfoot Field Researchers Organization. Last modified March 29, 1998. http://www.bfro.net/GDB/show_report.asp?id=6463.

Anonymous eyewitness. Untitled report about a sighting of a large wasp-like creature in San Bernardino, CA, 1992. Gulf Coast Bigfoot Research Organization. Accessed October 4, 2009. http://www.gcbro.com/WS0070.html.

Anonymous eyewitness. Untitled report about a sighting of an unusual giant man in Tangipahoa Parish, LA, November 1957. Gulf Coast Bigfoot Research Organization. Accessed December 24, 2004. http://www.gcbro.com/WS0018 .html.

Arment, Chad. "Giant Centipedes in the Ozarks." *North American BioFortean Review* 1, no. 2 (1999): 5–6.

Bethel, Brian. "The Black Eyed Kids." Creepypasta.com. Last modified August 06, 2008. http://www.creepypasta.com /the-black-eyed-kids/.

Bille, Matthew A. *Rumors of Existence: Newly Discovered, Supposedly Extinct, and Unconfirmed Inhabitants of the Animal Kingdom.* Blaine, WA: Hancock House, 1995.

Blackburn, Lyle. *Lizard Man: The True Story of the Bishopville Monster.* San Antonio, TX: Anomalist Books, 2013.

Bord, Janet, and Colin Bord. *Alien Animals.* Harrisburg, PA: Stackpole, 1981.

———. *Unexplained Mysteries of the 20th Century.* Chicago: Contemporary, 1989.

Carrington, Richard. *Mermaids and Mastodons: A Book of Natural and Unnatural History.* London: The Scientific Book Guild, 1961.

Clark, Jerome. *Unexplained!: 347 Strange Sightings, Incredible Occurrences, and Puzzling Physical Phenomena.* Detroit: Visible Ink, 1993.

Coleman, Loren. "Camel Spiders and Other Alleged Giant Spiders." *Cryptomundo* (blog), November 11, 2010. http://cryptomundo.com/cryptozoo-news/giantspiders-4/

———. *Curious Encounters: Phantom Trains, Spooky Spots, and Other Mysterious Wonders.* Winchester, MA: Faber and Faber, 1985.

Coleman, Loren, and Jerome Clark. *Cryptozoology A to Z: The Encyclopedia of Loch Monsters, Sasquatch, Chupacabras, and Other Authentic Mysteries of Nature.* New York: Fireside, 1999.

Coleman, Loren, and Patrick Huyghe. *The Field Guide to Bigfoot, Yeti, and Other Mystery Primates Worldwide.* New York: Avon Books, 1999.

Colvin, Sydney. "The Gigantic Wuhnan Toads." *Cryptid Chronicles* (blog), May 5, 2013. http://cryptidchronicles .tumblr.com/post/49748230085/the-gigantic-wuhnan -toads-an-isolated.

Cryptozoology News. "Fisherman Spots Giant Spider in Missouri River." *Cryptozoology News*, December 29, 2013. http://cryptozoologynews.com/fisherman-spots-giant-spider-missouri-river/.

Davis, M. K. "M. K. DAVIS Interview and Discussion with MIGFOOT BOOKS, This Being PART ONE." *BIGFOOT'S bLOG*, November 30, 2009. http://bigfootbooksblog .blogspot.com/2009/11/m-k-davis-interview-and -discussion-with.html.

Dinsdale, Tim. *The Leviathans*. London: Routledge & Kegan Paul Ltd., 1966.

Dong, Paul. *China's Major Mysteries: Paranormal Phenomena and the Unexplained in the People's Republic*. San Francisco: China Books and Periodicals, 2000.

Floyd, E. Randall. *Great Southern Mysteries*. Little Rock, AR: August House, 1989.

Freeman, Richard. *Dragons: More than a Myth?* Exeter, UK: CFZ Press, 2005.

———. *Orang-Pendek: Sumatra's Forgotten Ape*. North Devon, UK: CFZ Press, 2011.

Gerhard, Ken. *Big Bird!: Modern Sightings of Flying Monsters*. Bideford, UK: CFZ Press, 2007.

———. "San Antonio's Shadowy Hat Man Spooks Residents." *San Antonio Current*, January 20, 2012. http://www .sacurrent.com/Blogs/archives/2012/09/14/san-antonios -shadowy-hat-man-spooks-residents.

Godfrey, Linda S. *American Monsters: A History of Monster Lore, Legends, and Sightings in America*. Los Angeles: Tarcher, 2014.

Gordon, Stan. *Astonishing Encounters: Pennsylvania's Unknown Creatures, Casebook 3*. Greensburg, PA: 2015.

Gosse, Philip H. *Romance of Natural History*. London: James Nisbet & Co, 1860.

Gould, R. T. *The Loch Ness Monster and Others*. London: Geoffrey Bles, 1934.

Gross, Patrick. "June or July 1955, Loveland, Ohio, USA, Carlos Flannigan." UFO Related Entities Catalog. Last modified February 14, 2008. http://ufologie.patrickgross.org/ce3/1955-usa-loveland.htm.

Hall, Mark A. *Natural Mysteries: Monster Lizards, English Dragons and Other Puzzling Animals*. Bloomington, MN: Mark A. Hall Publications, 1991.

———. *Thunderbirds: America's Living Legends of Giant Birds*. New York: Paraview Press, 2004.

Heuvelmans, Bernard. *In the Wake of the Sea-Serpents*. New York: Hill and Wang, 1969.

———. *On the Track of Unknown Animals*. New York: Hill and Wang, 1959.

Heuvelmans, Bernard, and B. F. Porchnev. *L'homme de Néanderthal est toujours vivant*. Paris: Librairie Jules Tallandier, 1974.

Jenelle. "Thunderbird Sighting Boulder, Co." Cryptozoology .com. Accessed November 25, 2007. http://www .cryptozoology.com/sightings/ (site discontinued).

Kirk, John. "Alaskan Cadborosaurus Preview Now Available." *Cryptomundo* (blog), July 18, 2011. http://cryptomundo .com/cryptotourism/alaskan-caddy/.

———. *In the Domain of the Lake Monsters: The Search for Denizens of the Deep.* Toronto: Key Porter Books, 1998.

Krantz, Grover S. *Bigfoot Sasquatch Evidence.* Blaine, WA: Hancock House, 1999.

Lewis, Chad. *Hidden Headlines of Texas: Strange, Unusual, & Bizarre Newspaper Stories 1860–1910.* Eau Claire, WI: Unexplained Research Publishing Co, 2007.

Mackal, Roy P. *The Monsters of Loch Ness.* London: Macdonald and Jane's, 1976.

———. *Searching for Hidden Animals: An Inquiry into Zoological Mysteries.* London: Cadogan Books, 1980.

Marlowe, Scott. *The Cryptid Creatures of Florida.* North Devon, UK: CFZ Press, 2011.

Mausó, Pablo Villarubia. "The Mysteries of Honduras," *Inexplicata* 4 (Fall 1999). http://www.geocities.ws /INEXPLICATA2000/issue4/5.html.

Melimom. Comment on "Loveland Frog" by Craig Woolheater. *Cryptomundo* (blog), January 27, 2007. http://cryptomundo.com/bigfoot-report/loveland-frog/.

Miller, Marc E. W. *The Legends Continue: Adventures in Cryptozoology.* Kempton, Illinois: Adventures Unlimited, 1998.

Myrkle Jr., William Gregory. "Flying Humanoids on Coast to Coast." *Cryptomundo* (blog), September 7, 2013. http://cryptomundo.com/cryptozoologists/flying-humanoids -on-coast-to-coast/.

Newitz, Annalee. "In Mexico, chupacabras are blamed for 300 goat beheadings." *io9* (blog), September 1, 2010. http://io9 .gizmodo.com/5627117/in-mexico-chupacabras-are -blamed-for-300-goat-beheadings.

Oudemans, A. C. *The Great Sea Serpent.* With an introduction by Loren Coleman. New York: Cosimo Classics, 2007.

Paust, Gil. "Alaska's Monster Mystery Fish." *Sports Afield Magazine,* January 1959.

Plambeck, Steve. *The Loch Ness Giant Salamander* (blog). http://thelochnessgiantsalamander.blogspot.com/.

Pourcher, Abbé Pierre. *The Beast of Gevaudan: La Bête du Gévaudan.* Translated by Derek Brockis. Bloomington, IN: AuthorHouse, 2006.

Rabinowitz, Alan. J*aguar: One Man's Struggle to Establish the World's First Jaguar Preserve.* New York: Arbor House, 1986.

Redfern, Nick. *Chupacabra Road Trip: In Search of the Elusive Beast.* Woodbury, MN: Llewellyn Publications, 2015.

———. *Monster Files: A Look Inside Government Secrets and Classified Documents on Bizarre Creatures and Extraordinary Animals.* Pompton Plains, NJ: New Page Books, 2013.

Rosales, Albert. "Humanoid Sighting Reports & Journal of Humanoid Studies." Ufoinfo.com. Accessed October 9, 2008. http://www.ufoinfo.com/humanoid/.

Sanborne, Mark. "An Investigation of the Duende and Sisimite of Belize: Hominoids or Myth?" *International Society of Cryptozoology* 11 (1992): 90–97.

Sanderson, Ivan T. *Abominable Snowmen: Legend Come to Life.* Philadelphia: Chilton Co., 1967.

———. "The Missing Link?" *Argosy Magazine,* May 1969.

Shackley, Myra. *Still Living?: Yeti, Sasquatch, and the Neanderthal Enigma.* New York: Thames and Hudson, 1983.

Shuker, Karl P.N. *From Flying Toads to Snakes with Wings: From the Pages of FATE Magazine*. St. Paul, MN: Llewellyn, 1997.

———. "A Giant Mystery Salamander from California, and a Giant Very Sillymander from Vietnam." *ShukerNature* (blog), May 20, 2015. http://karlshuker.blogspot .com/2015/05/a-giant-mystery-salamander-from.html.

———. *In Search of Prehistoric Survivors: Do Giant 'Extinct' Creatures Still Exist?*. London: Blandford, 1993.

———. *A Manifestation of Monsters: Examining the (Un)usual Suspects*. San Antonio, TX: Anomalist Books, 2015.

Strickler, Lon. "Dinosaurs Run Amok in South Texas Town?" *Phantoms and Monsters* (blog), October 7, 2013. http:// www.phantomsandmonsters.com/2013/10/dinosaurs-run -amuck-in-south-texas-town.html.

———. "Was It The Frogman…Or Something Else Lurking In Loveland, Ohio?" *Phantoms and Monsters* (blog), December 14, 2011. http://www.phantomsandmonsters .com/2011/12/was-it-frogmanor-something-else-lurking .html.

Stringfield, Leonard H. "Evidence in the Flesh—The Gnomen." In *Inside Saucer Post … 3-0 Blue: CRIFO Views the Status Quo; A Summary Report*, 65. Online reproduction of the 1957 Cincinnati edition by National Investigations Committee on Aerial Phenomena, 2007. http://www.nicap .org/books/3-0Blue/InsidesaucerPost3-0Blue.htm.

Tralins, Robert. *Supernatural Strangers*. New York: Popular Library, 1970.

Whitcomb, Jonathan. Live Pterosaur. Accessed April 14, 2012. http://www.livepterosaur.com/.

Wright, Bruce. "Fresh evidence that Alaska's Illiamna lake monster is a Pacific sleeper shark? (+VIDEO)." *Alaska Dispatch News*, June 23, 2012. http://www.adn.com/article /fresh-evidence-alaskas-iliamna-lake-monster-pacific-sleeper-shark-video.

INTERIOR ART CREDITS

Illustrations on pages 12, 72, 96, 153 and 172 by Meg Buick.

Photo on page 22 by Steve Busti.

Photos on pages 32, 36, 52, 67, 81, 91, 105, 110, 121, 122, and 164 provided by the author.

Illustration on page 42 by RobRoy Menzies.

Illustration on page 139 by Ismael Wylie.

Illustration on page 184 by Thomas Finley.

Illustration on page 199 by Sam Shearon.

To Write to the Author

If you wish to contact the author or would like more information about this book, please write to the author in care of Llewellyn Worldwide Ltd., and we will forward your request. Both the author and publisher appreciate hearing from you and learning of your enjoyment of this book and how it has helped you. Llewellyn Worldwide Ltd. cannot guarantee that every letter written to the author can be answered, but all will be forwarded. Please write to:

Ken Gerhard
℅ Llewellyn Worldwide
2143 Wooddale Drive
Woodbury, MN 55125-2989

Please enclose a self-addressed stamped envelope for reply,
or $1.00 to cover costs. If outside the U.S.A., enclose
an international postal reply coupon.

GET MORE AT **LLEWELLYN.COM**

Visit us online to browse hundreds of our books and decks, plus sign up to receive our e-newsletters and exclusive online offers.

- • Free tarot readings • Spell-a-Day • Moon phases
- • Recipes, spells, and tips • Blogs • Encyclopedia
- • Author interviews, articles, and upcoming events

GET SOCIAL WITH **LLEWELLYN**

**Find us on
Facebook**

www.Facebook.com/LlewellynBooks

Follow us on

www.Twitter.com/Llewellynbooks

GET BOOKS AT **LLEWELLYN**

LLEWELLYN ORDERING INFORMATION

Order online: Visit our website at www.llewellyn.com to select your books and place an order on our secure server.

Order by phone:
- • Call toll free within the U.S. at 1-877-NEW-WRLD (1-877-639-9753)
- • Call toll free within Canada at 1-866-NEW-WRLD (1-866-639-9753)
- • We accept VISA, MasterCard, American Express and Discover

Order by mail:
Send the full price of your order (MN residents add 6.875% sales tax) in U.S. funds, plus postage and handling to: Llewellyn Worldwide, 2143 Wooddale Drive Woodbury, MN 55125-2989

POSTAGE AND HANDLING

STANDARD (U.S. & Canada):
(Please allow 12 business days)
$30.00 and under, add $4.00.
$30.01 and over, FREE SHIPPING.

INTERNATIONAL ORDERS:
$16.00 for one book, plus $3.00 for each additional book.

Visit us online for more shipping options.
Prices subject to change.

FREE CATALOG!

To order, call
1-877-
NEW-WRLD
ext. 8236
or visit our
website

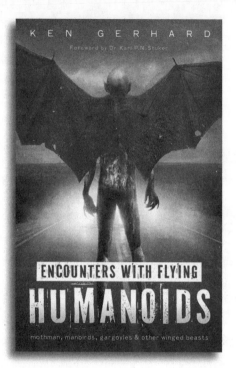

KEN GERHARD

Foreword by Dr. Karl P. N. Shuker

ENCOUNTERS WITH FLYING

HUMANOIDS

mothman, manbirds, gargoyles & other winged beasts

Encounters with Flying Humanoids
Mothman, Manbirds, Gargoyles
& Other Winged Beasts
KEN GERHARD

A strange creature with gigantic, blood-red embers for eyes crept out of the dark in West Virginia. Dozens of witnesses reported seeing the winged beast—later identified as the Mothman—take flight, chasing cars at speeds exceeding 100 miles per hour.

Cryptozoologist Ken Gerhard has traveled the world collecting evidence on the Mothman, the Owlman, the Van Meter Creature, the Valkyrie of Voltana, the Houston Batman, and other strange "bird people" that have been sighted throughout history. Packed with famous historical cases and dozens of chilling first-person accounts, this is the first book to focus exclusively on flying humanoids—a wide array of airborne entities that seem to "feed off our fear like psychic vampires."

978-0-7387-3720-1, 240 pp., 5 ³⁄₁₆ x 8 $14.99

EXPLORING THE MYTH & DISCOVERING THE TRUTH

BIGFOOT

TOM BURNETTE & ROB RIGGS

Bigfoot
Exploring the Myth & Discovering the Truth
Tom Burnette and Rob Riggs

Over the past twenty years, two men from different parts of the United States have followed and developed a friendly connection with the mysterious ape-like creature known as Bigfoot. Now, with forty-plus years of combined field study, these experienced investigators present a detailed collection of personal stories, ethnographic research, and theories surrounding the Bigfoot legend.

Join authors Rob Riggs and Tom Burnette, whose many years of commitment to the search and dedicated study reveal their true encounters with the elusive, wild being. Explore the history, habitats, and more in this collection of substantial evidence of Bigfoot's existence and thought-provoking discussions for continued research. From the possibility of having psychic powers to why it's so hard to find, *Bigfoot* goes beyond the myth to the reality of this amazing ape-man.

978-0-7387-3631-0, 264 pp., 5 ³⁄₁₆ x 8   **$15.99**

CHUPACABRA
ROAD TRIP

in search of the
elusive beast

Nick Redfern

Chupacabra Road Trip
In Search of the Elusive Beast
NICK REDFERN

In 1995, Puerto Rico was seized with mass hysteria over a new menace lurking in the rainforests, gruesomely killing livestock, leaving strange holes in their necks, and draining their bodies of blood. Described by eyewitnesses as a devilish creature three feet tall with spikes along its back and a mouth full of razor-sharp fangs, the strange animal was given the name Chupacabra—Spanish for "goat sucker."

Join noted monster hunter Nick Redfern and his spirited crew as they traverse the rugged backcountry of Puerto Rico, Mexico, and Texas investigating the continuing legacy of this fearsome beast. Whether he's interviewing locals, analyzing physical evidence, or sorting out the facts from the legends, Nick's journey into the realm of the Chupacabra will make you wonder just what's out there lurking in the night.

978-0-7387-4448-3, 264 pp., 5 ¼ x 8   **$15.99**

GARY GILLESPIE
chronicles of the
unexplained
True Stories of Haunted Houses,
Bigfoot & Other Paranormal Encounters

Chronicles of the Unexplained
True Stories of Haunted Houses, Bigfoot & Other Paranormal Encounters
GARY GILLESPIE

Open your eyes and mind to bizarre, bone-chilling encounters with creatures and places that, officially at least, don't exist. This unforgettable collection showcases ordinary people who have experienced a brush with the freakish realm. Featuring Bigfoot, skinwalkers, dark entities, and even a haunted piece of land with the terrifying ability to make things disappear forever, *Chronicles of the Unexplained* is filled with true events that defy any attempts at explanation.

Told with a keen eye for historical detail and a genuine appreciation of the natural (and unnatural) world, the original accounts in this fascinating book come from the Midwestern rail yards, the oil fields of North Dakota, the old mining towns of Colorado, and beyond. These frightening, entertaining, and inspiring tales prove that there are still plenty of mysteries in this world to explore.

978-0-7387-4538-1, 216 pp., 5 ³/₁₆ x 8　　　　　　　　**$15.99**

JOHN MICHAEL GREER

MONSTERS

10th Anniversary Edition
Revised & Expanded

AN INVESTIGATOR'S GUIDE TO MAGICAL BEINGS

Monsters
An Investigator's Guide to Magical Beings
John Michael Greer

Of course that monster hiding under your bed when you were little didn't really exist. Vampires, werewolves, zombies, demons —they're simply figments of our imagination, right? After all, their existence has never been scientifically proven. But there is one giant problem with such an easy dismissal of these creepy creatures: people keep encountering them.

Join occult scholar John Michael Greer for a harrowing journey into the reality of the impossible. Combining folklore, Western magical philosophy, and actual field experience, *Monsters: An Investigator's Guide to Magical Beings* is required reading for both active and armchair monster hunters.

This tenth anniversary edition of the quintessential guide to magical beings features a new preface, new chapters on chimeras and zombies, and updates on werewolves, dragons, and the fae.

978-0-7387-0050-2, 312 pp., 7 ½ x 9 ⅛   **$19.95**
